Mauritius

WORLD BIBLIOGRAPHICAL SERIES

General Editors:
Robert G. Neville (Executive Editor)
John J. Horton

Robert A. Myers   Ian Wallace
Hans H. Wellisch   Ralph Lee Woodward, Jr.

John J. Horton is Deputy Librarian of the University of Bradford and currently Chairman of its Academic Board of Studies in Social Sciences. He has maintained a longstanding interest in the discipline of area studies and its associated bibliographical problems, with special reference to European Studies. In particular he has published in the field of Icelandic and of Yugoslav studies, including the two relevant volumes in the World Bibliographical Series.

Robert A. Myers is Associate Professor of Anthropology in the Division of Social Sciences and Director of Study Abroad Programs at Alfred University, Alfred, New York. He has studied post-colonial island nations of the Caribbean and has spent two years in Nigeria on a Fulbright Lectureship. His interests include international public health, historical anthropology and developing societies. In addition to *Amerindians of the Lesser Antilles: a bibliography* (1981), *A Resource Guide to Dominica, 1493–1986* (1987) and numerous articles, he has compiled the World Bibliographical Series volumes on *Dominica* (1987), *Nigeria* (1989) and *Ghana* (1991).

Ian Wallace is Professor of German at the University of Bath. A graduate of Oxford in French and German, he also studied in Tübingen, Heidelberg and Lausanne before taking teaching posts at universities in the USA, Scotland and England. He specializes in contemporary German affairs, especially literature and culture, on which he has published numerous articles and books. In 1979 he founded the journal *GDR Monitor*, which he continues to edit under its new title *German Monitor*.

Hans H. Wellisch is Professor emeritus at the College of Library and Information Services, University of Maryland. He was President of the American Society of Indexers and was a member of the International Federation for Documentation. He is the author of numerous articles and several books on indexing and abstracting, and has published *The Conversion of Scripts* and *Indexing and Abstracting: an International Bibliography*. He also contributes frequently to *Journal of the American Society for Information Science, The Indexer* and other professional journals.

Ralph Lee Woodward, Jr. is Chairman of the Department of History at Tulane University, New Orleans, where he has been Professor of History since 1970. He is the author of *Central America, a Nation Divided*, 2nd ed. (1985), as well as several monographs and more than sixty scholarly articles on modern Latin America. He has also compiled volumes in the World Bibliographical Series on *Belize* (1980), *Nicaragua* (1983), and *El Salvador* (1988). Dr. Woodward edited the Central American section of the *Research Guide to Central America and the Caribbean* (1985) and is currently editor of the Central American history section of the *Handbook of Latin American Studies*.

VOLUME 140

Mauritius

Pramila Ramgulam Bennett
Compiler
with the collaboration of
George John Bennett

CLIO PRESS
OXFORD, ENGLAND · SANTA BARBARA, CALIFORNIA
DENVER, COLORADO

British Library Cataloguing in Publication Data

Bennett, Pramila Ramgulam
Mauritius. – (World bibliographical series v. 140)
I. Title   II. Series
016.96982

ISBN 1–85109–153–X

Clio Press Ltd.,
55 St. Thomas' Street,
Oxford OX1 1JG, England.

ABC-CLIO,
130 Cremona Drive,
Santa Barbara,
CA 93117, USA.

Designed by Bernard Crossland.
Typeset by Columns Design and Production Services Ltd, Reading, England.
Printed and bound in Great Britain by
Billing and Sons Ltd., Worcester.

THE WORLD BIBLIOGRAPHICAL SERIES

This series, which is principally designed for the English speaker, will eventually cover every country (and many of the world's principal regions), each in a separate volume comprising annotated entries on works dealing with its history, geography, economy and politics; and with its people, their culture, customs, religion and social organization. Attention will also be paid to current living conditions – housing, education, newspapers, clothing, etc.– that are all too often ignored in standard bibliographies; and to those particular aspects relevant to individual countries. Each volume seeks to achieve, by use of careful selectivity and critical assessment of the literature, an expression of the country and an appreciation of its nature and national aspirations, to guide the reader towards an understanding of its importance. The keynote of the series is to provide, in a uniform format, an interpretation of each country that will express its culture, its place in the world, and the qualities and background that make it unique. The views expressed in individual volumes, however, are not necessarily those of the publisher.

VOLUMES IN THE SERIES

Contents

Contents

Introduction

Mauritius gained independence on 12 March 1968 as a democratic country within the Commonwealth, with Her Majesty the Queen as Head of State. Despite general agreement among the political parties that Mauritius should adopt a republican constitution, two attempts to enact the necessary legislation have failed to win the requisite two-thirds majority support among members of Parliament. However, this has been more for party political than constitutional reasons. Mauritius, uniquely among members of the Organization of African Unity before the 1990s, successfully changed its government through democratic, multiparty elections after independence. It is a country with a plural but remarkably homogeneous society. Moreover, it has developed from a small nation with a large population, reliant on one cash-crop for its foreign exchange earnings – the 'overcrowded barracoon' in V. S. Naipaul's description – to one with a diversified and successful economy, with full employment.

The islands that form Mauritius lie in the southwest region of the Indian Ocean. The main island is called Mauritius and lies over sixteen hundred kilometres east of the African mainland and eight hundred kilometres east of the coast of the island of Madagascar. Mauritius, Réunion (a *département* of France) and Rodrigues (a dependency of Mauritius) form the Mascarene Islands. Other islands owned by Mauritius, are to the north, Agaléga and to the northeast, the Cargados Carajos group of islands, which includes St. Brandon, and the disputed Chagos Archipelago, which includes the atoll of Diego Garcia. The area of Mauritius is only 1,860 sq. km, that of Rodrigues 110 sq. km, and the other islands are even smaller.

Mauritius was formed by volcanic activity and the cones of extinct volcanoes rim the cool central plateau. The coast is hot and the climate as a whole is sub-tropical. The country has few natural resources except a fertile soil, good water supplies and a climate suitable for growing sugar cane, which is cultivated over nearly forty per cent of the land. Mauritius, Rodrigues and Agaléga lie in the path of cyclones that can cause extensive damage.

Introduction

The islands are isolated and are situated well away from regular shipping routes. There are frequent scheduled international flights to Mauritius but the outer islands are served only by ships or small aeroplanes and have limited contact with the outside world.

Mauritius was uninhabited for many years and was first discovered by Arab and Swahili seamen. The name *Dina mozare*, meaning Eastern Isle, appears on an early Arabic world map. The Portuguese visited Mauritius in the early 16th century and gave the name 'the Mascarenes' to the three islands of Mauritius, Réunion and Rodrigues, after the Portuguese navigator Pedro Mascarenhas. Nonetheless it was the Dutch who first settled in Mauritius, in 1598, naming the island after the *stadthouder*, or military chief, of the Union of Holland, Maurice of Nassau. The Dutch were – like the other European naval powers in the Indian Ocean at the time – more interested in trading than settlement, and Mauritius became a staging post for ships to call for food and water and repairs on their way to the east. The Dutch colony proved to be unsuccessful. The settlers plundered the forests, felling most of the island's ebony trees, introduced Java deer and rats, and exterminated the island's wingless dodo bird, only to abandon the islands, moving many of their people to their newer colony on the Cape of South Africa.

When, in 1710, the Dutch moved out, the French were already established in Madagascar, Bourbon (Réunion) and Rodrigues. The French had developed a successful coffee-growing industry on Bourbon and in 1715 Captain Dufresne d'Arsel, bringing the first coffee plants from Mocha on the Red Sea, put in at Mauritius, renamed the island the Ile de France and claimed it for his country. The new colony did not begin to prosper until the arrival, in 1735, of Mahé de La Bourdonnais, a thirty-six-year old Breton sea captain and a man of vision and ability. By the time he left Mauritius, eleven years later, the island's development was well advanced. Mauritius had become the administrative headquarters of the Mascarene Islands and French influence in the southwest Indian Ocean was firmly established. La Bourdonnais developed Port Louis as the island's main port and capital and the first sugar factory was opened under La Bourdonnais' governorship. Today his statue (along with that of Queen Victoria and various other French and English notables) still looks down on the Place d'Armes near the harbour in Port Louis.

La Bourdonnais did not succeed in permanently persuading the French East India Company to make Port Louis a free port, and over the next twenty years his four successors as governors operating under Company rule were preoccupied with the need to develop the island at a time of war between France and Britain. The difficulties suffered both by the inhabitants and the Company at this time eventually led to the sale of the island to the French crown in 1764. It also led to a rise in the number of pirates and corsairs – the latter having French backing for their raids on ships of other nations. From 1767 to 1788, under the new governors-general and intendants who now ran the island, the population doubled. First of the intendants – who were in charge of finance and justice – was Pierre Poivre, probably second only to La Bourdonnais in his contribution to the development of Mauritius. Under Poivre's administration the harbour services were improved, an engineering service, a pharmacy and a printing works established and flour mills, bakeries and warehouses to store flour and rice were built. Poivre's ambition to make the Ile de France a centre for growing spices did not materialize, but the island was important as a nursery for spices that were later grown successfully on other Indian Ocean islands. During the prosperous period of rule under the French monarchy, slaves were brought from the east coast of Africa and they eventually accounted for four-fifths of the population; previously, when the islands were under Company rule most of the slaves had come from Madagascar and some from West Africa, where the French East India Company had an island base off the coast of present-day Senegal. The slaves were treated badly and some escaped to live in the interior of the island. The *sega* dance and music, as well as other cultural features of present-day Mauritius, were brought to the island from Africa by the slaves.

In 1789 Bernardin de Saint-Pierre's romantic novel *Paul et Virginie* was published. At this time the Ile de France became the capital of all France's possessions east of the Cape, and Port Louis was a fashionably Europeanized city. The year 1789 also brought the French Revolution, the news of which did not reach the Ile de France until early in 1790. A period of some confusion followed but a Colonial Assembly was formed and gradually took over the responsibilities of governing the island. There were some Jacobins in the Ile de France who tried to gain ascendancy but with little success; of more account was the decision in France that slavery was to be abolished. The islanders rejected this decree and turned their attention to opposing the English naval attacks.

Subsequently Napoleon rose to power in France, and let it be known that he would not oppose the continuation of slavery in the Mascarene Islands. Napoleon sent Charles Decaen as governor. The Colonial Assemblies and the local councils then fell into abeyance as Decaen introduced the Napoleonic legal system (known as the Code Decaen) which still remains the basis of law in Mauritius today. There were also advances in education, fortifications were improved and social life flourished again. However, although corsairs – the most famous of them was Robert Surcouf – continued to raid British shipping, gradually the British naval blockade took effect.

The British captured the Ile de France in December 1810, following their seizure of Rodrigues and Bourbon, despite an early French success in defeating a British squadron. The British allowed the settlers to remain and respected their property, laws and customs for they were much more interested in securing the route to India than in colonizing the islands. Bourbon was returned to France because it did not have a good harbour and was considered of no value. The French cultural influence in Mauritius has remained strong ever since, despite the adoption of English as the main official language of education. An Act for the Abolition of the Slave Trade had been passed by the British Parliament in 1807 but the first British governor, Robert Farquhar, anxious not to lose the support of the settlers, whom he needed to help develop the island, did little to enforce this law. In 1833 under the Act for the Abolition of Slavery the British government finally provided compensation (amounting to more than two million pounds) to the slave owners, who invested the money in the sugar estates which had grown in prosperity following the decision by Britain to admit Mauritian sugar at the same rate of duty as West Indian sugar. The Act compelled the slaves in Mauritius to work as paid labourers on the sugar estates for four years following the abolition of slavery so that the planters had time to seek labour elsewhere and plantation owners looked to India for an alternative source of cheap labour.

By the mid-1850s Mauritius produced more sugar than any other country in the British Empire. Exports increased from 11,000 tons in 1823 to 121,000 tons in 1860, though after that time competition from other countries brought about a decline in production. The sugar industry was labour intensive and by 1909 when Indian immigration was halted nearly 450,000 indentured labourers had been sent to Mauritius – the majority of whom never returned to India. These indentured contract labourers had been preceded by skilled Indians, invited to the island by the French, and by convicts employed in road building, as well as slaves working as servants and on the land. The Mauritian plantation owners claimed that the Indian labourers were better off in Mauritius than in India but in fact they were poorly paid and were treated little better than slaves. Despite disquiet in England, little was done before the end of the 19th century to improve conditions for the Indian plantation workers. At the same time the Mauritians became stricken by diseases such as cholera, rabies and malaria, while several cyclones caused widespread destruction of crops and the flimsier houses.

During the 19th century the smaller islands of Agaléga, Cargados and the Chagos were administered by private individuals; Rodrigues produced salt fish, poultry and pigs, which it exported to Mauritius, but its population consisted of less than two hundred freed slaves and a few whites in the middle of the century.

With the invention of the steamship, communications with the rest of the world improved. A railway system (no longer in use today) was constructed and by the end of the century Mauritius was linked to Europe by an undersea cable. The construction of the Suez Canal had brought Europe even closer. However the sugar trade was declining, and, following labour problems, the poorer land was acquired by Indian smallholders for sugar cane production, making it even more difficult to diversify the agricultural base of the island. Although Mauritius acquired its first elected legislative council in 1885, the restrictive voting qualifications meant that the sugar plantation owners held on to their dominant position. The population of Mauritius steadily grew and by 1901 it had reached 371,023. Nonetheless, Mauritius continued to be severely affected by cyclones, malaria and other diseases, and in 1893 and 1896 there were disastrous fires in Port Louis.

During the First World War although shipping movements decreased, the price of sugar went up, so that Mauritius became relatively prosperous again. However, the island's workforce demanded better wages and the planters tried – only partially successfully – to recruit more labourers in India. Following the war the 'retrocession' movement, advocating the return of Mauritius to France, developed. The argument was that the cultural links were so strong that this was a logical step. The movement, however, came to nothing. Between the two World Wars, the labourers and the Indian sugar planters began to agitate for a better deal. Before the outbreak of hostilities in 1939 the Mauritius Labour Party had been established and had begun to organize strikes on the sugar estates. In this connection, it is interesting to recall that in 1901 Mahatma Gandhi had visited Mauritius and in 1909 a Royal Commission had recommended that agricultural co-operatives be set up.

The war brought air communications to Mauritius for the first time. These were established following the British retreat from Singapore after it was captured by the Japanese. By the end of the war, moves were in hand for a form of self-government for the islands. Helped by a malarial eradication scheme, the population was still increasing rapidly and was to reach a million by the mid 1970s. The Labour Party consolidated its political position following the introduction of universal human suffrage in 1958, and by 1965 plans for full independence were being made.

Sir Seewoosagur Ramgoolam led the Labour Party, allied with the

Independence Forward Bloc (IFB) and the Muslim Action Committee (CAM), to victory in the 1967 elections. The Parti Mauricien Social Démocrate (PMSD), led by Sir Gaëtan Duval, stood for a more limited independence than that proposed by the Labour Party, a kind of association with Britain which meant that Mauritians retained their British passports and which tied the economy closely to that of the United Kingdom. Sir Seewoosagur argued that this sort of quasi-independence would mean that Mauritius would not, for example, be able to approach the World Bank except through Britain; the Labour Party stood for full independence. Duval's policies attracted Creole and Franco-Mauritian votes, but he lost the election by a narrow margin. After gaining independence in 1968, however, riots between Creoles and Muslims resulted in a coalition government being formed by Ramgoolam between the Labour Party, the PMSD and the CAM.

Paul Bérenger, a Franco-Mauritian with radical ideas, emerged as the moving force behind the formation in 1969 of the Mouvement Militant Mauricien (MMM) which appealed to the younger voters. The MMM also supported trade unionists, in their campaign to form a new collective body, the General Workers' Federation (GWF), a coalition of eleven separate unions. The MMM was opposed to the close ties Mauritius maintained with South Africa and, in addition, also called for the return of Diego Garcia, which had been detached from Mauritius in 1965 and reconstitued with the title of the British Indian Ocean Territory. Subsequently the Territory had been partly leased to the US as a military base, with its inhabitants deported to Mauritius, although compensation was later paid by Britain. The MMM scored its first electoral success in 1970, winning a by-election in Ramgoolam's own constituency of Triolet. The government then legislated to postpone the general election – due in 1972 – until 1976, and to fill vacant seats with candidates from the same party. Alarmed by strikes in the early part of the year which were believed to have been instigated by Bérenger and his colleagues, and unnerved by the growing popularity of the MMM, the government banned public meetings and gave the police extra powers. A forty-day dock strike which started in September was followed by the declaration of a state of emergency in December. MMM leaders were detained which enhanced their support in the country, although now some differences were apparent between members of the party's hierarchy. The Prime Minister took control of the foreign affairs portfolio and launched a number of international initiatives, the most notable being the Organization of African Unity conference hosted by Mauritius in 1976, followed by his Chairmanship of the Organization. But economically, Mauritius was going into recession.

At the December 1976 general election the MMM won thirty-four seats, forcing a weakened Labour Party (twenty-eight seats) back into a coalition with the PMSD (eight seats), from which it had split after policy differences over tax and closer relations with France and South Africa, favoured by Duval.

In the 1982 elections the MMM, now in alliance with the new Parti Socialiste Mauricien formed by Harish Boodhoo in a split from the Labour Party, forced Sir Seewoosagur and Labour/PMSD out of office. The MMM/PSM won every seat in parliament, apart from the two seats for Rodrigues, which went to the Organisation du Peuple Rodrigais, whose MPs traditionally vote with the government and one of whom is appointed Minister for Rodrigues. Up to eight additional seats (apart from the sixty-two directly voted for) may be allotted on a 'best loser' basis by the electoral commission in order to preserve a balance between the different peoples of Mauritius. However, Mauritius's shaky economic position forced Bérenger, now Finance Minister, to go, in his own words 'cap in hand' to the International Monetary Fund and World Bank and the MMM's policies began to look less radical. Within a year, the politicians in the government quarrelled, and the Prime Minister, Aneerood Jugnauth, formed a new party (the Mouvement Socialiste Militant) while the MMM went into opposition. In 1983 Jugnauth won the general election in alliance with the Labour Party. However, strains developed within the government, and a split among the Labour members resulted in a new party, the Rassemblement des Travaillistes Mauriciens (RTM), being formed by those who continued to support Jugnauth. Despite MMM successes in local elections and drug scandals involving government MPs, Jugnauth hung on to power until August 1987 when his alliance won a clear majority under the MMM, now led by Prem Nababsing.

Jugnauth, now Sir Aneerood, had seen Mauritius begin to emerge during the 1980s as a country with a much sounder economy than Sir Seewoosagur Ramgoolam (who died in 1985) had inherited at independence. Tourism was flourishing, sugar was sold at good prices on a quota basis to the EEC under the Yaoundé Convention, and now there was a vital new addition to the country's revenues, which had been planned for a long time but taken time to come to fruition. This was the textile processing industry, making use of the abundant low-cost labour force on the island. The export processing zone factories were installed with inexpensive small-scale machinery, such as knitting and sewing machines, and used imported raw materials. Foreign businessmen were allowed beneficial tax concessions, a minimum of bureaucracy and generous help in setting up their enterprises. Before long Mauritius was one of the world's leading knitwear manufacturers, although there was not a solitary sheep on the island. By the end of the decade, Mauritius had full employment, a high standard of living, especially compared with most of its Indian Ocean neighbours. Indeed the country was held up as a unique example of prosperity and democracy in a region where many African countries seemed to have lost their way. Many people could claim credit for Mauritius's success but Jugnauth adroitly reaped the rewards, shedding first the PMSD and then the Labour Party from his alliance and going back to his old MMM colleagues in 1990 to form a new government. Although the new alliance between Jugnauth's renamed Mouvement Socialiste Militant and the MMM failed to bring in a republican constitution, it won a resounding victory at the polls the following year. The Labour Party, struggling to revive its fortunes under Dr. Navin Ramgoolam, Sir Seewoosagur's son, won three seats and the PMSD none at all in the 1991 election.

The bibliography

Books and archive material concerning Mauritius number many thousands and are found in many countries. Moreover, Mauritius was one of the earliest printing centres in the southern hemisphere and records of printed material originating in Mauritius itself date from 1768. In addition, the long and eventful history of Mauritius since its discovery as an isolated and uninhabited island has produced a large body of literature and many printed works, not only in English but also in French. Today there are 173 printing establishments on an island with a population of one million.

However, bibliographies of Mauritian literature are not new; work on comprehensive listings was carried out in the 19th century by Léon Doyen (1816-76), Prosper d'Epinay (1836-1914), Emile Daruty de Grandpre (1839-1903) and Albert Rae (1857-1919). The catalogues of the material they collected are vital for research into written material about Mauritius.

Later in the 20th century, Auguste Toussaint, the Chief Archivist of Mauritius, and his assistant, H. Adolphe, compiled a bibliography of Mauritius and its dependencies covering the *Printed record, manuscripts, archivalia and cartographic material, 1502-1954*. This major work, recording some 8,000 of the estimated 10,000 separate items then extant, was published in 1956.

In compiling this new bibliography although I have had to be selective, I have tried to include the most important, up-to-date and authoritative works. I do not attempt a comprehensive listing of the thousands of volumes and items currently available, but have brought together all those that I believe are of importance in order to give a vivid and accurate picture of the island as it is today. I have included a number of early manuscripts, mainly dealing with Indian immigration. The bibliography also lists a selection of early maps which are fascinating in themselves and are more consistent in showing Mauritius and the other small Indian Ocean islands than some modern atlases.

Each entry in the bibliography is accompanied by an annotation designed to guide the general reader, the student, researcher or businessman, as well as the specialist, through the different aspects of the country. All entries have been selected for their information on the island, either from a general perspective or because they focus on a particular subject, or lead on to further research. Cross references direct the reader to related works on a particular subject. Most chapters have a section listing general works, followed by specific books under separate sub-headings, e.g., the main chapter, History, is followed by sub-chapters dealing with 'general' works and then the Dutch, French and British periods and the modern pre- and post-independence eras. Although Diego Garcia is currently a disputed territory, I have included it as an integral part of Mauritius because it has always been administered from Mauritius and has been part of the country throughout most of its history.

Many important books written in French have been included. Mauritius was administered as a colony by France for many years and the French cultural influence remains strong. Accordingly, no bibliography of Mauritius can ignore the substantial volume of work on the island written in French. Where English editions of the French originals are available these have either been listed or referred to within annotations.

Within each section of the bibliography the books are listed alphabetically under their authors' names or title in the case of official publications. There is one fully integrated index, listing authors, subjects and titles alphabetically. In addition, there is also a glossary and a list of abbreviations and acronyms. All views expressed are those of the author, and any sins of omission or errors of fact are hers alone.

Acknowledgements

Grateful acknowledgement is made here to the following friends and colleagues who have contributed to the preparation of this bibliography by supplying information, helping to trace and assemble material and by making constructive suggestions. Particular thanks go to the hard work put in by Véronique Goessant and Babar Mumtaz of the Development Planning Unit, University College London; Indrani Gopauloo, Vijay Govinden, Yves Chan Kam Lon and Director Uttam Bissoondoyal of the Mahatma Gandhi Institute, Moka, Mauritius and Asha Burrenchobay, of the Ministry of Foreign Affairs, Port Louis, Mauritius. I wish also to thank Kate Cox, P. Sooprayen, Chief Archivist of Mauritius, K. Sowamber, Librarian of the Mauritius Institute, Raj Dassyne, Librarian of the University of Mauritius and Olga Louise, Library Officer, Vidu Nababsing, Surrendra Bissoondoyal, Director of the Mauritius Examination Syndicate and Chairman of Les Editions de l'Ocean Indien (EOI), Mrs D. Ramtohul and Miss S. Ramlallah of EOI; the staff of the City Library, Port Louis, the Carnegie Library, Curepipe, in Mauritius and the libraries of the School of African and Oriental Studies, the Commonwealth Institute, the Institute of Commonwealth Studies, the Royal Geographical Society and the Commonwealth Trust in London, Jacques Lee of Mauritian International, London and R. Chan Low; and also to His Excellency the High Commissioner for Mauritius in the United Kingdom, Dr Boudhun Teeluck and his staff.

Finally, I would like to thank Sir Harry Tirvengadum, Chairman, and the staff of Air Mauritius for enabling me to travel to Mauritius to undertake research for this book.

Pramila Ramgulam Bennett
London
29 September 1991

Glossary

Communal	Religious and ethnic groups, often with a political base.
Creole	The mother tongue of most Mauritians; also refers to people of African descent and mixed origin. Spelt Kreol in written Creole.
Dependencies	Islands that were administered from Mauritius.
Ilois	'Islanders' in Creole; since the 19th century has been used for the inhabitants of the Chagos Islands.
Ile de France/ Isle de France	The name given to Mauritius by the French.
Indentured labourers	Labourers bound by contract to a master; refers mainly to the workers brought from India to work on the Mauritian sugar-cane plantations.
Mascerene/Mascarenhas Islands/Mascareignes	The name given to the islands of Réunion, Mauritius and Rodrigues by the Portuguese navigator Pedro Mascarenhas.
Namasté	The traditional Hindu greeting by joining both palms below the chin; incorporated into Creole.
Plural society	Society containing several ethnic groups.
Retrocession	The 1920s movement promoting Mauritius's return to France.
Revision movement	The late 1920s movement demanding constitutional change.
Rodriguez/Rodrigues	Part of independent Mauritius, given the name of Rodriguez by its discoverer, Diego Rodriguez.

Glossary

Sega   The music and dance form unique to the Indian Ocean islands. The root of the word is from the Bantu language meaning 'play' or 'dance'.

Abbreviations and Acronyms

CAM	Comité d'action musulman (political party)
CEE	Communauté économique européenne
EOI	Editions de l'Océan Indien
EPZ	Export Processing Zone
IFB	Independence Forward Bloc (political party)
MA	Mauritius Archives
MCA	Mauritius College of the Air
MGI	Mahatma Gandhi Institute
MLP	Mauritius Labour Party
MMM	Mouvement Militant Mauricien (political party)
MSIRI	Mauritius Sugar Industry Research Institute
MSM	Mouvement Socialiste Militant (political party)
PMSD	Parti Mauricien Social Democrate (political party)

The Country and Its People

1 **Mauritius/The problems of a plural society.**
Burton Benedict.   London: Institute of Race Relations, 1965. 72p. map.
A useful account of the origins of Mauritius's peoples, the organization and social
structures that developed on the island, and later political developments. This book is
required reading for an understanding of Mauritian politics and society.

2 **The island of Rodriguez. A British colony in the Mascarenhas group.**
A.J. Bertuchi.   London: John Murray, 1923. 117p.
This study covers the history, geography, administration, climate, flora and fauna and
lifestyle of the inhabitants of the period. Written from a colonial perspective, the book
is an intriguing account of Rodrigues up to the 1920s, and contains some illustrations.

3 **Mauritius. Democracy and development in the Indian Ocean.**
Larry W. Bowman.   Boulder, Colorado: Westview Press, 1991. 208p.
maps. bibliog.
This is a good reference book about contemporary Mauritius. It outlines the political
history in the pre-independent days, and makes a very detailed study of the
development in the post-independence era. The author explains in his analysis the
unique combination of economic and political developments which have made the
island one of the most successful industrializing Third World countries. The island's
political culture, stability and economic policy changes with the establishment of the
free zone, textile and tourist industries are fully covered. Bowman's own revealing
interviews with members of the Mauritian political and economic élite are the basis for
this excellent introduction to independent Mauritius.

The Country and Its People

4 **Indian Ocean, five island countries.**
Edited by Frederica M. Bunge. Washington, DC: Foreign Area Studies, American University, 1983. 304p. maps. bibliog.

A book dealing individually with five independent Indian Ocean countries (Madagascar, Mauritius, The Comoros, Seychelles and The Maldives), followed by a chapter dealing with their interrelationships and relations with littoral and big-power countries. The section on Mauritius (chap. 2, p. 127-66) is dealt with, like the others, in political and economic terms and in the context of its struggle to survive with a fragile economy and culturally mixed population. Appendices, glossaries and an index are included.

5 **Islands of the Indian Ocean – Iles de l'Océan Indien.**
Gerald S. Cubitt, translated into French by Charles du Ray, Antoinette de Leon Silvestri. Cape Town; Johannesburg: C. Struik, 1975. 176p. maps.

This book introduces the islands of the Western Indian Ocean – Réunion, Mauritius, Madagascar, Seychelles and Comoros – through beautiful coloured and black-and-white pictures (234 in all) and vivid descriptive notes. History, topographic features, population, vegetation, monuments, beaches, lagoons, reefs and sea sports, gardens and other places of interest are some of the items dealt with. It is basically intended for the visitor, with the text in English and French side by side on the same page.

6 **Recueil de documents pour servir à l'histoire de Rodrigues.** (Collection of documents for the writing of Rodrigues's history.)
J.F. Dupon. Port Louis: R. Coquet, Imprimerie Commerciale, 1969. 120p. maps. (Mauritius Archives Publication, no. 10).

A collection of documents and extracts covering the period from the end of the 17th century to 1968, giving a useful account of Rodrigues's history during this time. The book, listing the documents in chronological order, covers the geography of the island, the increase in its population, its flora and fauna, and the slow pace of colonization.

7 **L'Ile Maurice aujourd'hui.** (Mauritius today.)
Jean-Pierre Durand, with the collaboration of Hervé Masson. Paris: Les Éditions Jeune Afrique, 1983. 199p. maps.

This richly illustrated book, written in French, presents a comprehensive panorama, covering the origins of the island, human settlements and post-independence Mauritius. It provides a perceptive description of Mauritian society with sensitive details, and also covers flora and fauna, marine life, the economy, and the arts and music. The island is placed on the world map, and a brief description is given of each town and place of interest. A chapter on Rodrigues offers useful tips and general information for the visitor. The fifty-eight colour pictures are by the artist Pierre Argo.

8 **Mauritius – Maurice.**
Régis Fanchette. Port Louis: Mauritius Government Tourist Office, [n.d.].

In English and French under the same cover, and with rich illustrations, this book presents Mauritius to its visitors. History, geography, religion, flora and fauna, and the economy are all briefly discussed in this well-informed introduction to the island.

2

9 **Mauritius: stepping into the future.**
Régis Fanchette, Pierre Argo.   Stanley, Rose Hill, Mauritius: Editions
de l'Océan Indien, 1988. 184p.

Richly illustrated in colour, this book is by two well-known Mauritians; Fanchette is a
writer, poet and journalist and Argo, who is responsible for the photographic coverage
and layout, is a painter. It contains useful information about the people, their customs,
cuisine and festivities. There is also a section on the island's recent economic
developments including its road network, education, housing, tourism and the
industrial explosion.

10 **The Mauritius handbook.**
M.K. Gundoa.   Port Louis: Government Printing Office, 1989. maps.

A brief but complete description of the many different facets of Mauritius – its
geography, history, major institutions, economy and culture. A few chapters are
devoted to Rodrigues as well. This factual book, published by the Ministry of
Information, is primarily intended as a basic guide and reference work for the visitor.
It is abundantly illustrated with colour plates giving a vivid idea of its physical,
economic and cultural landscapes. Statistics for 1988 are included.

11 **Ile Maurice.** (Mauritius.)
W. Edward Hart.   Port Louis: General Printing & Stationery, 1921.
128p. bibliog.

Though also useful for studies in human geography and ethnography, this book is
intended for the general public. Hart includes historical accounts of Dutch and French
settlements, delves into the origin of place-names, and describes the beauty spots and
natural curiosities together with the myths, legends and popular beliefs of his time.

12 **Standard encyclopedia of the world's oceans and islands.**
Anthony Huxley.   New York: G.P. Putnam's, 1962. 324p. maps.

This encyclopedia includes a description of Mauritius as well the other island groups in
the Indian Ocean. A brief note on location, area, land, people and government for
each country is backed by a gazetteer and an index.

13 **Madagascar, Mauritius and other East-African islands.**
C. Keller.   London: Swan Sonnenschein & Co. Ltd, 1901. 242p. maps.
bibliog.

A complete and authentic scientific study of Madagascar, Mauritius and the other
smaller islands of the Indian Ocean to the east and south-east of Africa. Chapter XVI
deals with Mauritius, its geographical position, its geology, coral reefs, settlements and
communications. The Mascarenes are dealt with in a global context. The geologist,
botanist, zoologist, meteorologist, ethnologist as well as the historian will find the work
of considerable interest. The maps are in colour, with sixty-four other illustrations in
black-and-white.

14 **Mauritius: the development of a plural society.**
    A. Ramoutar Mannick. Nottingham, England: Spokesman, 1979.
    174p. map. bibliog.

The book tries to give a comprehensive picture of the historic and political development of the island starting with its discovery, French settlement and English colonial history, and emphasizing population structure and social mobility. The government's attempts to tackle the economic problems posed by its previous dependence on the sugar industry, together with the constitutional advance made through the emergence of political parties and independence, are described in detail.

15 **Mauritius.**
    In: *Africa Contemporary Record.* Edited by Colin Legum. London:
    Africana Publishing Company, New York: Holmes & Meier, 1968/69–.
    annual.

An invaluable yearly review of Africa with detailed statistical information and authoritative introductory notes on individual countries, organizations and themes. In the 1986-87 edition, Mauritius appears on p. B367-B378, and an overall picture of the political, economic and social situation can immediately be had by reading these pages. There is also a statistical survey including figures on population, income and employment. This is a reliable and quick reference book.

16 **Mauritius.**
    In: *The African Review 1990/91.* Saffron Walden, England: World of
    Information, 1991. 232p. maps.

The review includes a short account of Mauritius (p. 137-140) covering tourism, the economy and the economic outlook, politics, external relations and a business guide. Some statistics are included and Mauritius's strong economy is referred to in the chapter entitled 'Africa in 1990: year of turmoil'.

17 **The economic and social structure of Mauritius. Report to the governor of Mauritius.**
    James Edward Meade (et al.) London: Methuen, 1961. 246p. maps.
    (Sessional Paper no. 7 of 1961, Port Louis).

This is a report to the Governor of Mauritius published by authority of the Mauritius Legislative Council. It contains the comprehensive findings of a commission set up in 1959 to survey the economic and social structure of Mauritius and recommend action to maintain and improve the standard of living of its people. Tables are included, with an appendix on forestry as an important secondary industry.

18 **Islands.**
    Henry William Menard. New York: Scientific American Books, 1986.
    215p. map.

A good deal of general information, as well as scientific and historical data, is included about the Indian Ocean islands and Mauritius in this comprehensive survey of the world's island territories. The study also examines the geographical formation of the islands and their discovery. A three-page map shows the location of the world's islands.

19 **The overcrowded barracoon and other articles.**
V.S. Naipaul. London: André Deutsch, 1972; Penguin Books, 1976.
312p.

The 'overcrowded barracoon' refers to Mauritius, and is the title of the last essay in this collection. Naipaul's article, first published in the *Sunday Times* in 1972, paints a vivid picture of an island in the grip of depression at a time when unemployment was high. The author met both politicians and ordinary people, and discusses the philosophy of Paul Bérenger's 'Mouvement Militant Mauricien' (MMM).

20 **The island of Mauritius.**
Raymond Philogène. Port Louis: General Printing & Stationery, Esclapon, 1928. 74p.

Factual, informative and of interest to the general reader, the book gives a brief account of the island's geography, history and population; its political, economic and social activities are also dealt with. Sports, religion and education are looked into in some detail. It is available at the Mauritius Archives and other public libraries.

21 **Limuria: the lesser dependencies of Mauritius.**
Robert Scott. Oxford: Oxford University Press, 1961. 308p. maps. bibliog.

An attempt to draw a picture of small, remote islands of the western Indian Ocean and of their inhabitants. The author sailed among the islands, so much of the book is based on firsthand information. It covers the Chagos Archipelago, which includes Diego Garcia, Agaléga and St. Brandon. This lively, readable account encompasses history, geography and social conditions, and is illustrated with black-and-white photographs. It is written with serious interest, and includes a useful bibliography.

22 **Mauritius – its people, its culture.**
S. Selvon, I. Asgarally, A. Unnuth. [Port Louis]: Editions Arc-en-Ciel, 1988. 90p.

This book satisfies the basic curiosity of the visitor to Mauritius. It gives clear answers to questions about its peoples, culture, legends, languages and religions. What makes it different from other guides is the mention of books by Mauritian authors that are of interest, and it also tells the visitor, for instance, where to buy a painting by a Mauritian artist. There are many colour illustrations.

Geography

General

23 **Descriptive account of Mauritius, its scenery, statistics, with a brief historical sketch preceded by elements of geography (the latter designed for youth).**
John Anderson.   [Port Louis]: The Author, 1858. 140p. map.
An intriguing account of Mauritius in the mid-19th century, written for 'families and schoolchildren' and 'with a brief historical sketch preceded by elements of geography'. It emphasizes such elements of life in Mauritius at the time as schools and holidays and is notable for the light it sheds on colonial society, the British influence and its geographical descriptions.

24 **A school geography of Mauritius.**
R.H. Ardill.   Port Louis: Ag Government Printer, 1957. 3rd ed. 49p. maps.
Though basically written for primary-school pupils aged seven to twelve years, this book is interesting to a much wider public. It describes the island's location, climate, forest, agriculture, population and communications. The island's dependencies, as other islands administered from Mauritius, and some of which now make up independent Mauritius, were known before 1968, and neighbours are also integrated into the study. There are several diagrams.

25 **The peaks of Limuria.**
Sir Hilary Blood.   In: *Geographical Magazine*, vol. 29, no. 10 (1957), p. 516-22.
A description of Rodrigues and Diego Garcia by a former governor of Mauritius (1949-54); it includes photographs taken on Diego Garcia in the mid-1950s. Limuria refers to the lesser (smaller) dependencies, also sometimes called the peaks of Limuria because they are believed to be the visible parts of a submerged continent.

26 **Primary geography for Mauritius.**
   C.E. Brown, J.C. Hockey, L.C. Vellin.   London: Longman, 1966. 63p.
   maps.

A pupils' book, aimed at giving a basic geographical education to five to twelve year
olds. It gives a brief description of the island's topography, climate, land-use patterns
(agricultural and industrial), population, settlement and communications. The
neighbouring islands are also introduced. The illustrations are by Hans Schwarz. No
longer in use in primary schools, as geography does not figure as an independent
subject on the curriculum, it is now available only in public libraries.

27 **Géographie illustrée de l'Ile Maurice et de Rodrigues.** (An illustrated
   geography of Mauritius and Rodrigues.)
   S.B. de Burgh Edwards.   Port Louis: General Printing & Stationery,
   1921. 42p. maps.

A brief description of Mauritius's location, extent, topography, climate, vegetation,
natural resources, demography and government, with an even more brief description
of the dependencies. The approach to the study of geography is a traditional one;
however, the information on communication, commerce, imports and exports and the
working of government institutions is useful. There are several illustrations.

28 **Nouvelle géographie à l'usage des écoles de l'Ile Maurice.** (New
   geography for Mauritian students.)
   A. Canot.   Port Louis: Imprimerie du Cernéen, 1841. 479p.

Though about 'cosmography', and more of a textbook on world regional geography,
this book is of relevance. In line with contemporary teaching of geography, it reveals
much about the teaching and learning methods and curriculum of the period, i.e. 19th-
century Mauritius. Written in French, it can be consulted at the Mauritius Institute,
Port Louis.

29 **Collection of the Royal Society of Arts and Sciences of Mauritius.**
   Port Louis: Royal Society of Arts and Sciences, 1846–. annual.

The journal consists of a collection of miscellaneous papers and it has appeared
annually since 1846. The papers are in English and French and the 'journal' is
available at the Mauritius Archives. Besides letters and manuscripts on geology,
mineralogy, oceanography, travels and cartography, the documents in the collection
relate to industries, sugar cane and other topics. It contains a lot of information on the
flora and fauna of Mauritius and the neighbouring islands, and includes articles which
are papers presented by members and others at meetings of the society: e.g. 'Notes on
the flora and fauna of Round Island' read by Sir Henry Barkly on 30th Dec. 1870;
another paper entitled 'Notes on the flora of Flat Island' read by John Horne in 1886;
and 'Les réformes de la sucrerie coloniale' [Colonial reforms of the sugar industry] by
L. Ehrmann, 1886.

30 **La géographie par l'image et la carte.** (Geography through pictures and maps.)
Collège de Saint Joseph's Teachers.   Port Louis: La Typographie Moderne, 1930. 62p.

In French and English, this work was primarily intended for the primary-school Mauritian student of geography. Mauritius and its dependencies have pride of place in a general geography of the world. There are some historical details on Mauritius, and more than 100 illustrations in black-and-white.

31 **Geography of Mauritius and its dependencies.**
Nemours Decotter.   Port Louis: The Standard Printing Establishment, 1909. 31p.

This is an outline of the island's geographical location, extent, topography, climate, vegetation, population, economy and government. The information on the dependencies is scant. It is basically a book for children at primary-school level.

32 **An economic geography of the Commonwealth.**
Economist Intelligence Unit.   London; Glasgow: Blackie & Son Ltd., 1957. 296p. maps.

This book provides a concise account of the economic geography and potential of the Commonwealth, including Mauritius. The island's economy and natural resources are described at enough length to give an overall picture of the country in the mid-1950s.

33 **A geographical reader of Mauritius.**
Jules A. de Gaye.   Port Louis: Minerva Printing Establishment. 2nd ed. 1910. 59p. maps.

The book contains a brief history and geographical account of Mauritius, with the main focus being the author's attempt at correlating history and geography to show the strategic location of Mauritius in the Indian Ocean. The military weaknesses and strengths resulting from its topography are discussed with references to the capture of Mauritius in 1810.

34 **Remarks on the country, products and appearance of the island of Rodriguez, with opinion as to its future colonization.**
Edward Higgin.   *Journal of the Royal Geographical Society of London*, no. 19 (1849), p. 17-20.

The title describes the contents. It makes interesting comparison with A.J. Bertuchi's book on the island (q.v.) several decades later. Difficult of access and with no natural harbour, Rodrigues did not become fully colonized until after the mid-19th century.

35 **Ocean research index: a guide to ocean and fresh water research.**
Guernsey, Channel Islands: Francis Hodgson, 1970. 451p.

A collection of information on international organizations promoting research into marine and freshwater science. A list of museums and oceanographic centres, plus indices and bibliographies, are included. Mauritius's contribution to oceanic research is covered, as well as that of other Indian Ocean territories.

36 **Mauritius. A geographical survey.**
T. Ramdin. London: University Tutorial Press Ltd., 1969. 64p. maps. bibliog.

After a brief description of the island's location, relief, climate and natural vegetation, there follows a detailed analysis of the role of agriculture in the economy, the industrialization process, urbanization and demography. The author stresses the need for town and country planning with a view to conserving scarce resources. The work is illustrated with seventeen black-and-white photographs and contains fifteen maps and a number of diagrams.

37 **Le découverte des Iles Mascareignes.** (The discovery of the Mascarene Islands.)
Georges de Visdelou-Guimbeau. Port Louis: Esclapon, General Printing & Stationery, 1948. 65p. maps. bibliog.

This is a scholarly and well-documented work, written in French, which is of prime importance to geographers and historians, and which also makes fascinating reading for the general public. The author argues well the case that the Portuguese navigator, Pedro Mascarenhas, was not the discoverer of the Mascarene Islands, namely Mauritius, Réunion and Rodrigues. He substantiates his research with several cartographic documents and additional information from travel and exploration accounts. In the attempt to discover the exact dates on which the islands were discovered, the maps are scrutinized, the islands' position by latitude and longitude measured, all methodically and scientifically within the scope of the social sciences. The book carries a preface by the Mauritian historian, Auguste Toussaint, and a portrait of Don Pedro Mascarenhas as frontispiece.

38 **Narrative report: *Anton Bruun*, cruises V and VI.**
Woods Hole Oceanographic Institution. Woods Hole, Massachusetts: Woods Hole Oceanographic Institution, International Indian Ocean Expedition News Bulletin [n.d.], Cruise V, 6p. map; Cruise VI, 4p. map.

The US Program in Biology undertook two cruises in order to collect information about the ecology and biology of the western Indian Ocean. Cruise VI covered the western Indian Ocean and, starting from Bombay, went south to Mauritius and from there to Durban in South Africa.

The island of Rodriguez. A British colony in the Mascarenhas group.
See item no. 2.

Physical

39 **Anciens volcans de l'Ile Maurice.** (Ancient volcanoes of Mauritius.)
    France Dupavillon.   Port Louis: Mauritius Printing, 1964. 62p. maps.

This is an excellent piece of work in French which examines the physical relief of Mauritius and the way in which this was formed. The interpretation involves some geometric knowledge which is no obstacle to its readability. The work contains four maps and ten black-and-white plates.

40 **A case study of coastline erosion, and an assessment of beach stability at Flic-en-Flacq.**
    P. Gopaul.   BSc dissertation, University of Mauritius, 1990. 128p.

This paper is included here because it shows local concern for the environment. It is well-researched and looks at the conditions prevailing at one of the most popular beaches of the island.

41 **Physical and regional geography: Mauritius and its neighbours.**
    S. Maudhoo.   Port Louis: Esclapon, 1953, 79p. maps.

This standard reference book aims at explaining the influences of geographic, economic and political factors on the development of the region and focuses on the relationship between climate and sugar cane cultivation, the main agricultural industry of Mauritius. The physical and human geography of Rodrigues is also discussed. The work contains a number of diagrams as well as six maps.

42 **The geology and mineral resources of Mauritius.**
    E.S.W. Simpson.   London: HMSO, 1951. 217-238p.

This work was reprinted from *Colonial Geological and Mineral Resources*, vol. 1, no. 3. It investigates the geological aspects of the island, its volcanic origin, soils and land utilization in relation to the welfare scheme and its implementation. Also contained are the preliminary results of the geological survey undertaken by the Department of Geology, University of Cape Town, for the British Colonial Government as part of the British Government Colonial Development and Welfare Scheme.

Mountains of Mauritius.
See item no. 86.

Human/political

43 **Rose-Hill, la ville qui se souvient.** (Rose Hill remembers.)
Liliane Berthelot. Port Louis: Port Louis Diocese, 1990. 81p. maps.
bibliog.

This book, written in French, is concerned with the demographic character and residential as well as economic patterns of the town, which can trace its beginnings to the British colonial period. The personalities that helped to shape its present character are also covered. The work is illustrated with five plans of the town demonstrating the successive stages of its development. There are also two maps of Mauritius showing the distribution of the population and internal migration. In addition there are eight plates depicting personalities and monuments. This is a well documented and informative volume.

44 **La grande rivière de Port Louis.** (Grand River North West.)
Léon Huet de Froberville. Port Louis: General Printing & Stationery, 1922. 69p.

An insight into the social history of one of the most ancient settlements of the island, describing its origin, growth, population and activities. For many years, the waters of the Grand River North West were the nucleus of life for the settlement. A graphic image is built up by the description of the geographical location of the river and bay, their state in the dry and rainy seasons, the bridges, and the dams and habitation around it. This study, written in French, is an important contribution to the written history and geography of the country. There are six beautiful black-and-white photographs.

45 **Trou d'Eau Douce.**
Laurence Nairac. Port Louis: Précigraph, 1980. 8p.

With a preface by Edouard Maunick, Mauritian poet, this is a short history in French of the coastal village of Trou d'Eau Douce, its geological formation, geography, human settlements and economic activities. The book contains several photographs which reflect the village's present popularity with tourists.

46 **Vacoas-Phoenix, la génèse d'une ville.** (Vacoas-Phoenix, the genesis of a town.)
Sydney Selvon. Port Louis: Municipality of Vacoas-Phoenix, Swan Printing, 1984. 176p. maps.

A basic and valuable contribution to historical geography, in particular to the history of settlements and their growth and emergence as urban areas. It outlines the historical, economic and social factors that favoured the emergence of the twin-settlements of Vacoas-Phoenix. The process of inland migration is fully analysed. Six plans of the twin towns and statistical tables of population, 1901-31, complete the study. The book is written in French by a well-known Mauritian journalist and writer.

11

47 **Port Louis: a tropical city.**
Auguste Toussaint.   London: George Allen & Unwin, 1973. 144p.
maps. bibliog.

This book is an historical account of the city's foundation from 1735 to 1969, of its development as Mauritius's capital city and principal port and commercial centre. Statistical information and photographs complete this two hundred years' survey. It was first published in French by the Presses Universitaires de France in 1966 and later translated by W.E.F. Ward.

Meteorology

48 **Climate in Mauritius.**
Meteorological Services.   Vacoas, Mauritius: Meteorological Services Authority, 1972. 299p.

A detailed, technical study of the macro- and microclimates of Mauritius. The rainfall regime, wind systems and cyclones, humidity and insolation are discussed. It provides useful information for the farmers.

49 **Cyclone handbook.**
Port Louis: Government Printer, 1955. 19p.

An official booklet about cyclones, giving details of their climatic characteristics. This is an important publication because of the role cyclones play in the life of Mauritians. Illustrated.

50 **Climate atlas of the Indian Ocean – Part III.**
Stefan Hastenrath, Lawrence L. Greisher.   Madison, Wisconsin:
University of Wisconsin Press, 1990. 273p. maps.

The third part of this atlas, written in the light of the more detailed information available and with the help of more sophisticated weather instruments and techniques, deals with the upper hydrosphere of the tropical Indian Ocean within which zone of study Mauritius falls. It contains maps of temperature at standard depth levels from the surface to 400 metres, seasonal maps of salinity currents, ocean heat and vertical temperature profiles. Together with Parts I and II published in 1979, it is a valuable contribution to the study of islands' and oceans' climates, and is especially relevant to the western Indian Ocean where cyclones are frequent in the summer months (October to April).

51 **La pluie à Maurice.** (Rainfall in Mauritius.)
Marc Herchenroder.   Port Louis: General Printing & Stationery,
Esclapon, 1935. 61p. maps.

A scientific study based on the analysis of data collected over sixty years, with observations of special interest to climatologists. Mauritius, an island cut off from the mainlands by vast stretches of ocean, makes an interesting climatic study. The book analyses the rainfall regime – periodicity, variability, dispersion and the effects of deforestation. It is written in French, with a foreword by Maxime Koenig, and contains sixteen tables of statistics.

52 **Meteorological observations and climatological summaries for Mauritius, Rodrigues and the outer islands.**
Vacaos, Mauritius: Mauritius Meteorological Services, 1951–. monthly.
A regular bulletin, it provides substantial detailed information on weather elements, including cyclones, in tabular and map forms. It also carries core studies of cyclones.

53 **Meteorology in Mauritius (1774-1974).**
Meteorological Services. Vacoas, Mauritius: Mauritius Printing, 1974. 33p.
This study covers the history of the Mauritian Meteorological Service from its origin, tracing the long tradition of research in this field carried out by specialists, as the island is situated at the heart of the cyclone zone.

54 **Weather and climate of Mauritius.**
B.M. Padya. Moka, Mauritius: Mahatma Gandhi Institute, 1989. 283p. maps. bibliog.
A very readable, detailed and scientific study of the broad-scale atmospheric motions which determine the weather in Mauritius, including an in-depth description of local conditions and the weather elements influencing them. Based on the scientific analysis of data, and written to contribute to the corpus of knowledge in this field, it answers some of the questions which students of environmental science are likely to ask. There are 100 maps, charts, diagrams and tables of statistics, as well as references at the end of each chapter, and an index.

55 **Reports of the meteorological services.**
Vacoas, Mauritius: Meteorological Services, 1851–. annual.
A brief summary of weather conditions, diurnal and seasonal, for the year. The mean annual temperature and rainfall are given in tabular forms. Drastic changes in weather, violent cyclones, unusual heavy rainfall and severe drought are explained, though briefly. Over half of the report is devoted to the administration of the department.

56 **Technical reports on the cyclone season of southwest Indian Ocean.**
Compiled by the Meteorological Services, Mauritius. Vacoas, Mauritius: Meteorological Services, 1986–. annual.
These reports are annual compilations of the recorded observations of cyclones by the technical staff of meteorological departments in the Southwest Indian Ocean. The cyclone season lasts from December to May and plays an important role in the life of the islanders. Such observations are therefore necessary for determining cyclonic patterns.

57 **An inquiry into the nature and course of storms in the Indian Ocean south of the equator.**
Alexander Thom. London: Smith & Elder, 1845. 346p.

A useful examination of hurricanes and other phenomena in the region around Mauritius by an author who was a British naval officer stationed in Mauritius in the mid-19th century. He observed the Rodrigues storm of 1843 and makes practical suggestions for avoiding the storms prevalent in that part of the Indian Ocean.

Maps and atlases

58 **Elementary atlas of Mauritius.**
Jérôme Arékion. Port Louis: General Printing & Stationery, 1947.

This short but comprehensive atlas contains thirteen maps, and is designed for schools. Copies of it are available at the Mauritius Institute and other libraries in Mauritius.

59 **Maps of Mauritius.**
Jérôme Arékion. Port Louis. General Printing & Stationery, Esclapon, 1937.

A series of fifteen educational maps showing districts, towns and villages, roads and railway lines, relief (mountains, lakes, rivers, capes, bays), islands and lighthouses around Mauritius, places of interest and, uniquely, the distribution of Roman Catholic churches in Mauritius. The author's intention was to present 'a modest work of simple information'. Maps are not drawn to scale, as they were primarily intended for use by pupils of the primary and elementary schools.

60 **The universal atlas.**
Atlas Publishing Company. London: Cassell, 1893.

This atlas includes a small inset map of both Mauritius and Réunion on p. 102 which indicates some of the more important towns and the highest mountain. It can be consulted at the Royal Geographical Society's map room in London.

61 **Atlas souvenir de l'Abbé de la Caille.** (A souvenir atlas of Abbé de la Caille.)
Mauritius Archives. Port Louis: Archives Publication Fund, 1953.

This is a collection of maps of Mauritius to 1854, also covering the Dutch period in the 17th century, some by Abbé de la Caille himself, others by cartographers using his scientific data. There are nine maps in all; the first three are manuscripts with one and two from 1638-1710, the third from 1721-25; the six others are printed ones. It also includes a portrait of de la Caille and describes his life history; he was a member of the Royal Academy of Sciences, a mathematician and astronomer. Written in French, this is of great interest to geographers and historians alike.

62 **Atlas of the British Empire throughout the world.**
John Bartholomew.   London: George Philip & Son, 1873.
Map eleven, entitled 'Smaller settlements in Africa and adjoining oceans', includes Mauritius, and Seychelles and the Amirante Islands. A copy exists at the Mauritius Archives in Coromandel.

63 **The Times atlas of the world.**
John Bartholomew & Son Ltd.   Edinburgh; London: Times Books, 1980. 227p.
A comprehensive edition, this is a useful general atlas for the general investigator. It contains maps of the entire Indian Ocean area (including Mauritius) with information about capitals, area, population size, mineral and agricultural resources. There is also a detailed insert of the island of Rodrigues.

64 **The comprehensive atlas and geography of the world.**
Walter Graham Blackie.   London: Blackie & Son, 1882.
This atlas includes a map of Mauritius on p. 42 which is approximately ten centimetres square and pinkwash in colour. It shows hills and rivers and some coastal prints.

65 **The Mauritius atlas.**
London: W. Collins & Sons, 1945.
An atlas of twenty-five maps for schools planned under the direction of a joint advisory board: K.H. Huggins (geographical); B.A. Workman (educational); J.M. Parnish (technical); J.C.B. Redfearn (cartographical). It is now out of print but available at the Mauritius Archives.

66 **East India pilot.**
A. Dalrymple.   London: The Author, 1794.
In Volume 1, facing map 79, is a chart of the north-west coast of Mauritius or Isle de France, 1738. Facing map 78 are four plans of Mahébourg, the south-east harbour of Mauritius, called Port Bourbon by the French. Map 77 is of l'Isle de France, 1753, by Nicolas Louis de La Caille, while map 78 is a plan of Port Louis in the Isle de France (Mauritius), 1775, by de Boisquenay.

67 **Carte de Maurice.** (Map of Mauritius.)
Lithographed by A. Dardenne.   Port Louis: The Author, 1862.
A map giving the location of the main sugar factories, the limits of the districts, roads and the now defunct rail network. The transportation of sugar was by rail in those days. The map can be consulted at the Mauritius Archives.

68 **Mauritius: plan of the districts of Moka and Port-Louis.**
A. Descubes, lithographed by William Crook.   Port Louis: Public Works Department, 1879.
An interesting historical map. Moka, which is not far from the capital, Port Louis, is a region with a cooler climate and many settlers took up residence there. Moka has outgrown its original district boundaries, but has remained a residential area.

69 **Geological map of Mauritius.**
London: E.S.W. Simpson & Ors, 1951.

A survey of the island's geology in 1949 by J.R. Tregiaga, E.S.W. Simpson and L.O. Nicolaysen. The map appears in E.S.W. Simpson's *The geology and mineral resources of Mauritius* (q.v.) and is based on scientific studies. Further information can be obtained from the *Geological-Geophysical atlas of the Indian Ocean*, edited by D.I. Khir (UNESCO, 1975).

70 **Mauritius or the Isle de France.**
Hydrographic Office. London: The Admiralty, 1879.

The corrections to this general map were last made in 1942. Toussaint found 168 general maps of Mauritius, including Rodrigues, the Chagos Archipelago and the Cargados Carajos Archipelago group, in the period up to 1954.

71 **Carte touristique 1:100 000: Ile Maurice.** (Tourist map 1:100 000: Mauritius.)
Institut Géographique National. Paris: IGN, 1978.

This map, which is useful both to the visitor and Mauritians, indicates the main places of interest, beaches and road network. A number of such maps are now available since the growth of the tourist industry.

72 **Madagascar et Mascareignes: carte générale.** (Madagascar and the Mascarene Islands: general map.)
Institut Géographique National. Paris: IGN, 1968.

The inset map of Mauritius is drawn to a scale of 1:500 000 but contains enough detail to be of interest.

73 **Victoria Regina atlas.**
W. and A.K. Johnston. Edinburgh: The Authors, 1897.

This is quite a large, sharp and clear map, mainly orange in colour, which appears on p. 129. It is interesting to look at and shows lakes and rivers and what appears to be the rail network.

74 **Select plans of the principal cities, harbours, forts in the world.**
John Luffman. London: John Luffman, 1801.

Mauritius is represented in this atlas, which was produced at a time of British–French struggle for supremacy in the Indian Ocean. Port Louis, an outpost of France, was a corsair base. In the last decade of the 18th century, it also became a frequent port of call for American ships.

75 **Ediclo road atlas of Mauritius.**
P.A. Guy Martin. Port Louis: Ediclo, 1990. 40p. maps.

Written in English and French under the same covers, this road map is very useful to visitors. It is easy to use and has a comprehensive road index and colour maps, all attractively presented. It is the first of its kind, and with the extensive building in recent years, a most useful publication even to the Mauritian.

76 **Plans, maps & charts (1502-1954).**
A. Toussaint, H. Adolphe. In: *Bibliography of Mauritius (1502-1954)*.
Port Louis: Esclapon for Government of Mauritius, 1956. 884p.

Toussaint, Mauritius's Chief Archivist, and his assistant listed 1,295 maps, plans and charts in chronological order in their bibliography, which was the first to provide a cartography of Mauritius. They include general maps and plans of Mauritius and its dependencies, regional and district maps, maps of the South West Indian Ocean, including nautical charts, and world maps which show Mauritius and its neighbouring islands. Details include the location of each map.

77 **Philip's atlas of Mauritius.**
Devi Venkatasamy (et al.). London: George Philip, 1991. 47p.

This recently published atlas of Mauritius is both comprehensive and elaborate in its presentation of the geographical, economic and social features of the islands that form independent Mauritius. It also contains information about other countries and places Mauritius in a global context. The cartography is of high quality.

78 **Map of Mauritius.**
Stanislas Pelte. Port Louis: R. de Spéville & Co., 1915.

One of the first maps of the island showing roads suitable for cars, drawn specially for the Mauritius almanac, 1915 (p. A30). S. Pelte worked in the Department of Public Works.

79 **Environmental studies atlas for Mauritius.**
A.C. Kalla. London: Macmillan, 1989. 49p. maps.

This book introduces the reader to the Indian Ocean islands with emphasis on physical, political and economic geography. There are also details of the geological formation, climate and water resources, population and land use patterns, all complemented by plans, statistics, maps and pictures. There is an index.

Climatic atlas of the Indian Ocean – Part III.
See item no. 50.

World atlas of agriculture.
See item no. 351.

Travel guides

80 **The traveler's Africa, a guide to the entire continent.**
Philip M. Allen, Aaron Segal. New York: Hopkinson & Blake, 1973. 949p. bibliog.

This guide for travellers in Africa includes information on Mauritius in its Indian Ocean section. The general material – in particular the glossary – includes useful background material on Africa and the Indian Ocean islands.

81 **Le guide émeraude – guide routier et touristique: Ile Maurice, 1988.**
(Emerald guide – 1988 road atlas and tourist guide of Mauritius.)
Aurore Ltd. Plaine Lauzun, Port Louis: Mauritius Stationery
Manufacturers, 1988. 151p. maps.

This is a travel guide to Mauritius with an introductory chapter on geography, history, population, religion and culture, languages and local music. There follows a list of useful information about hotels, organized tours, car hire, shopping and gastronomy. This guide includes a chapter on Rodrigues. There are street maps and lists of places of interest.

82 **Let's visit Mauritius.**
Marie Benoît. Basingstoke, England; London: Macmillan, 1987. 95p.
map.

A tourist guide which introduces Mauritius to the outside world and is also a book of general knowledge. Chapters cover briefly the island's geography, history, economy and the people's cultural life. Lavishly illustrated, it contains fifty colour plates.

83 **Mauritius guide with street maps.**
Chandranee K. Bhuckory. Rose Hill, Mauritius: Editions de l'Océan
Indien, 1989. 136p. maps.

This is a very useful practical guide for the Mauritian tourist, giving a very brief history and a geographical, social, economic and political description of the island. It provides help to the tourist who wants to discover the nooks and crannies of the island, and also covers the main towns and other facilities such as restaurants, hotels, clubs and embassies. As well as a comprehensive map of Mauritius, there are also street maps of every town on the island.

84 **Guide to Mauritius.**
Royston Ellis. Chalfont St. Peter, England: Bradt, 1988. 230p. maps.

A general guide for tourists, businesspersons and the independent traveller. There are appendices on hotels, useful phrases in Creole, and an index of place-names. Much of the information is still relevant, but more hotels and restaurants have opened in the years since publication.

85 **Traveler's guide to East Africa and the Indian Ocean.**
Gill Garb. London: I.C. Magazine, 1981. 240p. maps.

A basic guide to East Africa and the Indian Ocean islands aimed at the tourist and traveller, with much useful information about hotels, weather, local customs, food and currencies. As with all such books, some information is liable to date quite quickly, but the basic facts are sound.

86 **Mountains of Mauritius.**
Robert V.R. Marsh, with a preface by L.F. Edgerley. 123p. maps.

This is a climber's guide which introduces the visitor to the volcanic mountains and hills of Mauritius, while the Mauritian discovers a great deal about his environment and the scope for leisure. There are twenty-seven route maps, nineteen plates (one colour, eighteen black-and-white) and one general map of Mauritius. Unfortunately, there is no mention of the publishing house and date of publication.

87   **Mauritius in your pocket/Mauritius in tasca 1989.**
      Antonio Rolfini, translated from the Italian by Rosemary Garlick.
      Milan, Italy: System Bank, 1988. 512p. maps.
A pocket-size tourist guide, copiously illustrated, with an up-to-date and comprehensive account of all the facts the visitor to Mauritius needs to know. The book includes brief descriptions of the history and geography of Mauritius, its people, and the flora and fauna, as well as practical information about currency, shopping, sightseeing and the weather. There are sections on the outer islands and the book includes advertisements. In this Italian/English-language edition, the English translation is unidiomatic.

Mauritius – its people, its culture.
See item no. 22.

Travellers' Accounts

88 **Les voyages du chirurgien Avine à l'Isle de France et dans la mer des Indes au début du XIXe siècle.** (Voyages of the surgeon Avine to the Isle de France and the Indian Ocean at the beginning of the 19th century.) Grégoire Avine. Port Louis: Mauritius Archives Publications, 1961. 83p.

The manuscripts of Grégoire Avine, naval surgeon, which describe the societies encountered in the Western Indian Ocean, have been brought together in this publication by Decary. Avine's approach is a humanitarian one; his descriptions of the peoples he observed are those of an ethnographer, and his botanical and zoological observations are precise. Illustrations supplement the French text, and there is an index of names.

89 **Voyage à l'Isle de France.** (Voyage to the Isle de France.) Jacques Henri Bernardin de Saint Pierre. Paris: Merlin. 1773, 1776. 2 vols. 108p.

Bernardin de Saint Pierre visited the island and describes 18th-century Mauritius, its people and their customs here. Details of the flora and fauna as well as of its geography and the local industries and commerce give an overall view of life at the time. His visit was to inspire him with the idea for his novel *Paul and Virginie* (q.v.). A photocopy of this book exists in the Mauritius Archives.

90 **Voyages aux colonies orientales.** (Voyages to the Eastern colonies.) Auguste Billiard. Paris: Ladvocat, 1822. 486p. map.

This French book is of general interest and brings together the letters written to Count Montalivet from the Ile de France (Mauritius) and Bourbon (La Réunion) during the years 1817 to 1820. The letters describe the peoples and their customs, their history, geography, local institutions, agriculture and the commerce of the two islands, the first now independent, the second a French *département*. The book also contains a plan of

Port Louis and other illustrations. It is available at the Bibliothèque Nationale de Paris.

91 **Voyage à l'Ile de France, dans l'Inde et en Angleterre.** (Voyage to the Isle de France, India and Great Britain.)
   Pierre Brunet.   Paris: P. Mongie Aîne, 1825. 390p.

This book reads like a novel, and the author's narration of his visit to Mauritius in Chapter II (p. 19-36) is seen through the eyes of a doctor. Brunet was captured by the British during the battles that saw the island pass into British hands. The book can be found at the Bibliothèque Nationale de Paris.

92 **Journal historique fait au Cap de Bonne Espérance.** (Historical journal written at the Cape of Good Hope.)
   Abbé de la Caille.   Paris: Guillyn, 1763; Paris: Nyon, 1776. 384p.

This book, written in French, explains the island's strategic position in the 18th century. It also describes the inhabitants and country generally. Though the fuller details are about the Hottentots of Southern Africa and other Cape peoples, this book is still not to be missed in any study of the political and historical geography of Mauritius during the French period.

93 **The voyage of the Beagle.**
   Charles Darwin.   New York: Bantam Books, 1958. 439p.

A complete copy of Darwin's diary during the voyage of the *Beagle*, with an account of his visit to Mauritius and other Indian Ocean islands (p. 373-439). Darwin's observations on that voyage led to his theory of coral formations. The book was produced in paperback and is unabridged.

94 **Indian Ocean sleighride.**
   Steve Dolley.   *Yachting*, vol. 133, no. 3, (Mar. 1973), p.66, p.118-19.

Steve Dolley steered his yacht *Ghostrider* through the Indian Ocean from the Cocos (Keeling) Islands to Mauritius, meeting a variety of seas on the way, from flat calm to raging storms.

95 **Agaléga/Pte Ile.** (Agaléga/Small Island.)
   R.P. Roger Dussercle.   Port Louis: General Printing & Stationery, 1949. 284p. map.

This is a lively and picturesque traveller's account (in French) of these islands. Agaléga is the name given to two very closely situated small islands, nearly 950 kilometres to the north of Mauritius. They form part of Mauritius and are inhabited by fishermen and a guano-collecting community. It gives a detailed account of its discovery, geological formation, flora and fauna, coasts and climate and the emergence of settlements, its population and economic activities. There are fifteen black-and-white photographs. This book is of considerable interest as it is one of the few written about the islands.

96 **Archipel de Chagos en mission.** (Chagos Archipelago: on a mission.)
R. Dussercle.   Port Louis: General Printing & Stationery, 1934. 215p.
map.

Father R. Dussercle, a missionary of the Compagnie du Saint-Esprit, curate of Saint
François Xavier, Port Louis, on being appointed to the Chagos Archipelago, made the
voyage to these distant islands, situated some 1,200 km. north of Mauritius. Dussercle
writes a romantic, narrative account of his voyage on his boat *Diégo* through the small
islands of the Chagos Archipelago (which includes Diego Garcia). He includes a
number of Creole songs which the islanders sang at work and in the evening. The
themes of the songs and the Creole spoken there make interesting study for the
development of the language and for comparison with other islands.

97 **Islands time forgot.**
Lawrence G. Green.   London: Putnam, 1962.

The author views lonely islands through romantic eyes; his chapter on the Mascarenes
includes a colourful account of Mauritius, where he found a blend of 18th-century
Frenchmen, London policemen, Chinese shopkeepers and Indian labourers. He
describes a visit to Chinatown in Port Louis, and a visit to Rodrigues.

98 **Voyages à Pékin, Manille et l'Ile de France.** (Voyages to Peking, Manilla
and the Isle de France.)
De Guignes.   Paris; Imprimerie Imperiale, 1808. 3 vols. maps.

Written in French, this book relates the voyages undertaken between the years 1784
and 1801, and contains information fundamental to any study of the island's people,
geography and history. The author, who was appointed French consul to Canton in
1784, was a famous sinologist. The book has an atlas attached.

99 **The Beagle record: selections from the original pictorial records and
written accounts of the voyage of H.M.S. Beagle.**
Richard Darwin Keynes.   London; New York: Cambridge University
Press, 1979. 386p. map.

A large-format and beautifully illustrated account of Darwin's voyage on *H.M.S.
Beagle*, including an account of the ship's visit to Port Louis on 29 April 1836.

100 **Voyage à Rodrigues.**
J.M.G. Le Clézio.   Paris: Editions Gallimard, 1986. 137p.

An autobiographical account of the author's journey to Rodrigues in the footsteps of
his grandfather. Le Clézio tells the life history and describes the force behind the
undertaking of such a voyage. The account is subjective with many analytical
observations.

101 **Les îles soeurs ou le paradis retrouvé – La Réunion et Maurice 'Eden de la Mer des Indes'.** (The sister islands or paradise regained – Réunion and Mauritius 'Eden of the Indian Ocean'.)
Marius Leblond. Paris: Editions Alsatia, 1946. 251p.

This is an interesting and serious work in French. 'Sisters' in their geography and ethnography, the two islands provide the inspiration for this study in human geography. Accounts of travels to the islands are followed by descriptions of their geological formation, their flora and fauna and human settlements. The work is illustrated.

102 **Voyage dans les mers de l'Inde.** (Voyage in the Indian seas.)
Guillaume Legentil. Paris: Imprimerie Royale, 1779-81. 10 vols. maps.

The voyage related here spans over eleven years; it was undertaken on the King's order on the occasion of the passage of Venus in front of the sun on 6th June 1761 and 3rd June 1769. The author has noted down his astronomical and meteorological observations in the region, which includes Mauritius. Plates 11 to 14 refer to Mauritius. The work is available in ten volumes of photocopies at the Mauritius Archives, and makes fascinating reading.

103 **L'île d'Agaléga: notes et souvenirs.** (Remembering Agaléga.)
J.G. Lionnet. Paris: Challamel, 1924. 84p.

Situated nearly 1,000 km. to the north of Mauritius, the small and little-known island of Agaléga is part of Mauritius. It is inhabited by some 500 people whose occupation is mainly fishing, coconut- and guano-collecting. Captain Lionnet's account of the island is one of the few depicting life there in the past or present.

104 **Voyage pittoresque à l'Isle de France, au Cap de Bonne Espérance et à l'Ile de Ténérife.** (Picturesque voyage to the Isle de France, the Cape of Good Hope and Tenerife.)
M.J. Milbert. Paris: Imprimerie de Le Normand, 1812. Reprinted, Marseilles, France: La Fitte Reprints, 1976. 782p. maps.

A general description of the island, its geography, soil, vegetation, climate, population, customs and administration. The figures quoted are based on the 1801 and 1808 censuses. The book is in French and contains several illustrations which were made in the country by the author-artist.

105 **Darwin and the *Beagle*.**
Alan Moorehead. New York: Harper & Row; London: Hamish Hamilton, 1969. 280p. map. bibliog.

An account of Darwin's voyage as shown in his diary, including his visits to Mauritius and Bourbon (Réunion) to collect botanical and other specimens. It is written in an accessible style, and is abundantly illustrated.

106 **The voyage of François Leguat of Bresse to Rodriguez, Mauritius, Java and the Cape of Good Hope.**
Edited and annotated by Pasfield Oliver. New York: B. Franklin, 1966. 164p.

A reprint of the 1891 edition published by the Hakluyt Society, London (vols. 82-83), the book is a fascinating account of the voyage and adventures of François Leguat de la Fougère (1637-1735) and his visit to Mauritius. It has been transcribed from the first English edition of 1708 published by Bonwicke, W. Freeman, London.

107 **The shoals of Capricorn.**
F.D. Ommanney. London: Longmans, Green & Co., 1952. 322p. maps.

Essentially a traveller's tale of visits to the islands of Mauritius and Seychelles, the book emphasizes the picturesque. There is some social information, mainly based on the author's meetings with the islands' inhabitants and his own observations. The maps are inside the front and back covers, and there are some illustrations.

108 **Sub-tropical rambles in the land of the aphanapteryx.**
Nicolas Pike. London: Sampson Low, Marton, Low & Searle, 1873; Freeport, New York: Books for Libraries Press, 1972. 509p. map.

A picturesque traveller's account of the personal experiences, adventures and wanderings in and around the island of Mauritius by Pike, who was the US consul to Mauritius in 1872. His observations give a good insight into the life of the diverse elements constituting the society of the late 19th century. Line drawings illustrate the text.

109 **Westward from the Cocos: Indian Ocean travels.**
Coralie Rees, Leslie Rees. London: George G. Harrap, 1956. 268p.

An account of a journey from Darwin in Australia across the Indian Ocean – by way of Mauritius – to East Africa and south to South Africa. This is an anecdotal travel story illustrated with photographs in black-and-white.

110 **Voyage dans les quatre principales îles des mers d'Afrique.** (Voyage to the four main islands in the seas of Africa.)
Bory de Saint Vincent. Paris: Buisson, 1804. 3 vols. maps.

Three volumes and an atlas cover this voyage which is narrated in French. The author was appointed chief naturalist to Captain Baudin's expedition ordered by the French government in the ninth and tenth year of the Republic (1801 and 1802). The work contains important details about the island's topography, geology, climate, and flora and fauna. The atlas comprises fifty-eight plates and maps. A photocopy is available at the Mauritius Archives.

111 **Voyages aux Indes Orientales et à la Chine.** (Voyages to the East Indies and China.)
Pierre Sonnerat. Paris: Dentu, 1806. 4 vols. maps.

The voyages were undertaken on the order of King Louis XVI in the years 1774 to 1781, and their narration makes fascinating reading. The book contains details about the customs, religion, arts and science as practised by the Indians and Chinese in Mauritius and in other countries of the region. Written in French, it is well illustrated and contains an atlas.

Flora and Fauna

112 **Flora of Mauritius and the Seychelles.**
J.G. Baker. London: Reeve, 1877. 558p.
A description of the flowers, flowering plants and ferns found in the two islands. H.H. Johnston later wrote *Additions to the flora of Mauritius, as recorded in Baker's book* (Edinburgh: [s.n.], 1895. 28p.)

113 **Geographical guide to the floras of the world: an annotated list with special reference to useful plants and common plant names.**
S.F. Blake, A.C. Atwood. Washington, DC: [s.n.], 1942. 336p.
Part one of this directory includes the islands of the Indian Ocean.

114 **A guide to common reef fishes of the Western Indian Ocean.**
Kenneth Bock. London; Basingstoke: Macmillan Education Ltd., 122p. maps.
An introduction to the common reef fishes of the Western Indian Ocean which includes Mauritius's waters, the book describes and illustrates about 120 species that an average observer is likely to encounter in two hours quiet goggling at low tide. A further fifty allied species are described. All these fishes are common throughout the Western Indian Ocean and occur in shallow water from shoreline to a depth of about five metres; coral reef is their particular and special environment. The photographs are by J. Mackinnon and I. Took.

115 **A history of woods and forests in Mauritius.**
N.R. Brouard. Port Louis: J. Eliel Felix, Government Printer, 1963. 86p. bibliog.
Brouard starts with a description of the uninhabited island of Mauritius in the early 16th century when it was almost entirely covered with forests. He goes on to tell of the Dutch occupation when the forests were exploited and the timber, especially ebony, sold in Europe; the period of French rule when the first comprehensive legislation on

forestry was passed, and British rule, during which half the remaining forest plantations were destroyed in the violent cyclone of 1960.

116 **Poissons de l'Ile Maurice.** (Fishes of Mauritius.)
Alain Cornic. Stanley, Rose Hill, Mauritius: Editions de l'Océan Indien, 1987. 336p.

A comprehensive guide to the fishes of Mauritius and the Indian Ocean which seeks to give sufficiently detailed descriptions to enable the species to be easily identified. Names are given in Creole, French, English and German. There are a considerable number of photographs in colour.

117 **Fleurs rares des îles Mascareignes.** (Rare flowers of the Mascarene Islands.)
Francis Friedman. Paris: ORSTOM, 1988. 60p.

Friedman's study of the flowering plants of the Mascarene Islands goes back to 1970. In this luxurious edition, there are colour illustrations of some most beautiful and rare flowers, including wild orchids, that grow on these islands.

118 **La végétation de l'Ile Maurice.** (The flora of Mauritius.)
Joseph Guého. Stanley, Rose Hill, Mauritius: Editions de l'Océan Indien, 1988. 75p. maps. bibliog.

The book tells the history of the island's indigenous vegetation and those plants that are imported, going as far back as the Dutch period. The emphasis is on man's role in the conservation of the ecological equilibrium of nature. A whole chapter is devoted to the botanical names of the plants, and there is a full index. Six maps and several photographs, in colour as well as in black-and-white, illustrate this well-researched work, which does not lose its scientific importance though told in a language that is accessible to anyone interested in his/her botanical/horticultural inheritance. It is available in both English and French editions.

119 **Faune ornithologique ancienne et actuelle des Îles Mascareignes, Seychelles, Comores et des îles avoisinantes.** (Ancient and current bird population of the Mascarene and other neighbouring islands.)
René Guérin. Port Louis: General Printing & Stationery, 1940-54. 3 vols.

This comprehensive study of the bird population of Mauritius and other neighbouring islands extends over many years and was published in instalments.

120 **The dodo and kindred birds or the extinct birds of the Mascarene Islands.**
Masauji Hachisuka. London: Witherby, 1953. 250p.

This illustrated book is primarily about the dodo, a widely-known bird which is now extinct and which is closely associated with the image of Mauritius overseas.

121 **Guide sous-marin de la Réunion et de l'Ile Maurice.** (Guide to the submarine world of Réunion and Mauritius.)
M. Harmelin-Vivien. Papeete, Tahiti: Éditions du Pacifique, 1981. map.

This guide to the undersea world of Réunion and Mauritius is of general interest, and with a special appeal to underwater enthusiasts. The text is by Harmelin-Vivien and the photographs by C. Pétron.

122 **Dans les jardins de l'Ile Maurice.** (In the gardens of Mauritius.)
Axelle Lamusse. Port Louis: Imprimerie Commerciale, 1978. 68p. bibliog.

The author hopes with the publication of this short book (which is a collection of articles that appeared in the national daily *L'Express*) to enable both her compatriots and tourists to discover the island's flora, and to interest them in such a way as to promote its conservation. It deals with the more exotic flowers and plants, and relates their history and cultivation.

123 **Birds of Mauritius.**
Claude Michel. Rose Hill, Mauritius: Editions de l'Océan Indien, 1986. rev. ed. 60p.

The book contains brief details about the various species of birds to be found on the island; indigenous as well as migratory species are included. The birds' habitat, reproduction habits and food are described. There are many black-and-white as well as colour illustrations of the birds.

124 **Marine molluscs of Mauritius.**
Claude Michel, Seeta Takoor, Mahmood Coowar. Rose Hill, Mauritius: Editions de l'Océan Indien, 100p.

Numerous line-drawings and colour plates accompany the descriptions of the molluscs. The focus is on univalve shells and on the molluscs' habits, modes of life and points of interest. The text avoids technical terms, as the book is intended for the general reader to identify local shells easily to be found. There is an index as well as a list of the illustrations.

125 **The vindication of François Leguat.**
Alfred North-Coombes. Port Louis: Société de l'Histoire de l'Ile Maurice, 1979. 248p. map. bibliog.

A comprehensive appraisal of Leguat's treatise on the natural history of the island of Rodrigues. There is a chronology from 1510 to 1968 (the year of independence) with a useful appendix referring to Leguat's book (q.v.). An agronomist, North-Coombs attempts to separate reality from legend.

126 **Sir Seewoosagur Ramgoolam botanic garden.**
     W. Owadally.   Stanley, Rose Hill, Mauritius: Editions de l'Océan
     Indien, 1988. 45p. map.

The world-famous botanical garden at Pamplemousses is described in detail, and is a useful guide to the flora and fauna found there. A map of the garden is included. A French version is also available.

127 **A preliminary list of insects of Diego Garcia Atoll, Chagos Archipelago.**
     Washington, DC: Smithsonian Institution, 1981. 26p. bibliog.

A list of insects found on the Diego Garcia Atoll, under their scientific names, and including those imported by man to control the native species.

128 **Le jardin botanique de Curepipe.** (Curepipe botanical garden.)
     G. Rouillard, Joseph Guého.   Stanley, Rose Hill, Mauritius: Editions
     de l'Océan Indien, 1990. 76p. maps.

This book remains one of the most detailed surveys of the islands' flora. The garden at Curepipe was created in 1870 some twenty years before the town was established. The work provides interesting details of the plants to be found in the botanical garden and describes the history of Curepipe.

129 **Geography and ecology of Diego Garcia Atoll, Chagos Archipelago.**
     D.R. Stoddard, J.D. Taylor.   Washington, DC: Smithsonian
     Institution, 1971. 224p. map. bibliog.

The marine and coral as well as the land flora and fauna are examined in scientific detail in this book, which includes a history of human settlement on the atoll. It is illustrated with photographs and black-and-white figures, and there is a comprehensive bibliography.

Madagascar, Mauritius and other East-African islands.
See item no. 13.

Collection of the Royal Society of Arts and Sciences of Mauritius.
See item no. 29.

Voyage à l'Isle de France. (Voyage to the Isle de France.)
See item no. 89.

Les îles soeurs ou le paradis retrouvé – La Réunion et Maurice 'Eden de la Mer des Indes'. (The sister islands or paradise regained – Réunion and Mauritius 'Eden of the Indian Ocean'.)
See item no. 101.

Voyage dans les quatre principales îles des mers d'Afrique. (Voyage to the four main islands in the seas of Africa.)
See item no. 110.

Some medicinal plants of economic importance in Mauritius.
See item no. 356.

History

General

130 A new history of Mauritius.
John Addison, K. Hazareesingh. London; Basingstoke, England: Macmillan, 1984. 116p. maps.
Although written as a textbook for secondary-school pupils, this book is also of interest to the general reader as a brief, but comprehensive history which concentrates on the island itself, and its subsequent political development up to and beyond independence. Illustrated with simple maps and black-and-white photographs, the book is one of the few English-language histories of Mauritius.

131 Early place-names of Mauritius.
P.J. Barnwell. Port Louis: General Printing, 1957. 106p.
The information for this book was gleaned from the logs of ships which visited Mauritius after 1628, mostly during the French period (to 1810). Many of those names have survived to the present day.

132 The truth about Mauritius.
B. Bissoondoyal. Bombay, India: Bharatiya Vidya Bhavan, 1968. 246p. maps.
Bissoondoyal, a Mauritian who was educated at Calcutta University, provides a comprehensive and lively account of Mauritius's history up to the time of independence. He emphasizes the leading personalities who shaped the country's politics and culture, and dwells on links with India and other Indian Ocean territories. The book is illustrated, and has an index.

133 **Une île et son passé. Ile Maurice 1507-1947.** (An island and its past. Mauritius from 1507 to 1947.)
Antoine Chelin. Port Louis: Mauritius Printing, 1973. 465p.

A chronological retrospection of the major events in Mauritian history over four centuries, written in French. Details are kept to a minimum, but it is well researched and all the important events are there. There is a full list of the Dutch officials, French and British governors (1638 to 1948), the administrators of Rodrigues (1736-1971) and the French consuls on the island (1840-1968).

134 **Une île et son passé (supplément).** (A supplement: an island and its past.)
Antoine Chelin. Quatre Bornes, Mauritius: Imprimerie Michel Robert et Cie, 1982. 108p.

This supplement to the 1973 book by the same author, also in French, deals with more information on dates and people who headed governments and departments, including the presidents of the Chamber of Agriculture.

135 **Regards sur la vieille cité.** (A view of the old city.)
Alain Gordon Gentil. Port Louis: Best Graphics Ltd., 1986. 68p.

This is an overview of the old city of Port Louis in the late 1950s to the early 1970s. There are numerous photographs illustrating historical buildings, monuments and streets of the capital.

136 **They came to Mauritius/Portraits of the eighteenth and nineteenth centuries.**
Derek Hollingworth. Oxford, England: Oxford University Press, 1965. 176p. maps.

This lively collection of individual portraits is aimed at stimulating interest in the history of the island. The author has chosen a number of French and Englishmen, and included persons of other nationalities who visited Mauritius from the days of French colonialism.

137 **National monuments of Mauritius.**
Mauritius Institute. Port Louis: Government Printers, 1988. 158p.

Glimpses of the history of Mauritius can be had through the short descriptions of the monuments that adorn Port Louis, the capital. The book was published in the context of the year of cultural heritage. Numerous photographs illustrate it, and there is a useful index.

138 **La découverte des Mascareignes par les arabes et les portugais.** (The discovery of the Mascarenes by the Arabs and the Portuguese.)
Alfred North-Coombes. Port Louis: Société de l'Histoire de l'Ile de France, 1979. 175p. maps. bibliog.

An important contribution to the history of the Indian Ocean in the 16th century, and therefore to the early history of Mauritius, which with Réunion and Rodrigues form the Mascarene Islands.

139 **Ile Maurice, ancienne isle de France, fille de la révolution.** (Mauritius, former Isle de France, daughter of the revolution.)
Jean Georges Prosper. Ste. Croix, Port Louis: Proag Printing, 1989. 195p. bibliog.

This book describes the effects of the French revolution of 1789 on Mauritius, then a French colony. Its implications for the society, culture and politics of the island are presented in the context of its independence. This history of politics culminates in a picture of Mauritius as a model nation of tolerance and democracy. There are photographs of well-known political leaders in the 1970s.

140 **The Indian Ocean in superpower strategies.**
R. Bux Rais. Ann Arbor, Michigan: University Microfilms International, 1981. 298p. bibliog.

A PhD thesis from the University of California, Santa Barbara, written against the background of the Cold War, showing that both Russia and America had commercial reasons for confrontation in the Indian Ocean, as well as military ones. The situation of Mauritius is to be viewed in this context.

141 **Historical dictionary of Mauritius.**
Lindsay Rivière. Metuchen, New Jersey; London: Scarecrow Press, 1982. 172p. (African Historical Dictionaries, no. 34).

This dictionary provides statistical information about Mauritius, with tables on finance, governors, etc. For the most part it is arranged alphabetically under headings ranging from 'Saree' (long piece of cloth worn by women which comes from India) to 'Van Der Meersch, Jacob' (the third Dutch governor of Mauritius).

142 **L'Ile Maurice à travers ses villages.** (Mauritius through its villages.)
M. Sewtohul. Ste. Croix, Port Louis: The Author, 1990. 156p. bibliog.

This is in the main the history of Triolet village, a major human settlement and also an important political constituency, being that of the late Sir Seewoosagur Ramgoolam. It is worth reading from a sociological and historical point of view.

143 **Bulletin annuel de la Société de l'Histoire de l'Ile Maurice.** (Annual bulletin of the Historical Society of Mauritius.)
Société de l'Histoire de l'Ile Maurice. Port Louis: Historical Society of Mauritius, 1938–. annual.

A yearly publication containing articles in English and French. The focus in each issue is a main event in the country's history, for example, the first 100 years of the Mauritius sugar industry.

144 **History of the Indian Ocean.**
Auguste Toussaint, translated from the French by June Guicharnaud.
Chicago: University of Chicago Press; London: Routledge & Kegan
Paul, 1966. 292p. maps. bibliog.

An authoritative and definitive survey of the history of what Toussaint describes as the neglected ocean. This account of events from antiquity to modern times by one of the leading historians of the region covers a wide geographical area, from Egypt to South-East Asia, and from South Africa to Australia, and examines the developing conflict for power between the Europeans and the peoples of the East. Toussaint sets out the role played by Mauritius, the most important of the Mascarene group of islands, in the history of the Indian Ocean. The detailed chronology, together with the straightforward style and well-organized assembly of the material, ensures its place as a key work of historical reference. The French edition, *Histoire de l'Océan Indien*, was published by Presses Universitaires de France, 1961.

145 **History of Mauritius.**
Auguste Toussaint, translated from the French by W.E.F. Ward.
London; Basingstoke, England: Macmillan Education, 1977. 105p.
maps. bibliog.

Auguste Toussaint, whose French ancestors settled in Mauritius in 1795, is the best known historian of the region, and was head of the Mauritius Archives. This book describes the first visits to the island in the 8th century by Arab seamen, the Portuguese in the 16th and the short Dutch settlement, followed by a hundred years of French rule, until the English conquest of 1810. The island's development is described up to the time of independence in 1968, and Mauritius is discussed in the context of its regional and international importance.

146 **Historical relations across the Indian Ocean.**
UNESCO. Paris: UNESCO, 1980. 183p. bibliog. (General History of
Africa: Studies and Documents).

A collection of papers resulting from a UNESCO conference in Port Louis in July 1974. The three parts of the meeting dealt with the cultural and commercial contacts across the Indian Ocean, the settlement of Madagascar and other Indian Ocean islands, and Indian Ocean studies in general. Each paper has its own selective bibliography and the authors include suggestions for further study.

147 **Prisoners in paradise.**
Sheila Ward. Port Louis: Editions de l'Océan Indien, 1986. 62p.

An account of several political prisoners who were detained in Mauritius during the French and British administrations. They include the English explorer, Matthew Flinders, captured by the French and detained under Decaen's governorship (1803-10) and Reza Khan Pahlavi of Iran.

148 **Asian and African systems of slavery.**
James L. Watson. Berkeley, California: University of California
Press, 1980. 384p. bibliog.
A number of sections in this book refer to the Indian Ocean, and some specifically to
Mauritius. Chapter VI, 'Slavery and Indenture in Mauritius and Seychelles', is
especially relevant, but a number of other chapters discuss the transportation of slaves
across the Indian Ocean and the subsequent cultural mix that resulted in present-day
Mauritius.

Ile Maurice. (Mauritius.)
See item no. 11.

Mauritius: the development of a plural society.
See item no. 14.

La découverte des Iles Mascareignes. (The discovery of the Mascarene
Islands.)
See item no. 37.

La grande rivière de Port Louis. (Grand River North West.)
See item no. 44.

Port Louis: a tropical city.
See item no. 47.

The development of education in Mauritius 1710-1976.
See item no. 403.

**Statistique de l'Ile Maurice et ses dépendances (suivie d'une notice historique
sur cette colonie et d'un essai sur l'île de Madagascar).** (Statistics of Mauritius
and its dependencies, followed by a short history of Mauritius and an essay
on Madagascar.)
See item no. 475.

The Dutch settlements (1638-58, 1664-92)

149 **The Dutch seaborne empire, 1600-1800.**
Charles R. Boxer. New York: Alfred A. Knopf, 1970; London:
Hutchinson, 1972. 294p. 326p. maps. bibliog.
An illustrated and detailed account of Dutch mercantile influence worldwide, with
many references to the Indian Ocean area and a chronology. Boxer examines the
foundation of the forts and factories which made up the Dutch East India Co. that had
such a profound impact throughout the Indian Ocean, including Mauritius, in the 17th
and 18th centuries.

150 **Pirates of the eastern seas, 1618-1723.**
Charles Gray. New York; London: Kennikat Press, 1971. 336p.

In the 17th and 18th centuries the Indian Ocean was notorious for the pirates who attacked merchant shipping and had their bases on the various Indian Ocean islands, including Mauritius. The pirates, who came from Denmark, Holland and England, were often covertly supported by their governments, and this book, which was first published in 1933, discusses this aspect of piracy as well as providing an account of the careers of the best-known of the pirate leaders of the time, including Sir Robert Rich, Dick Chivers and John Taylor.

151 **Manuscripts and archivalia 1598-1954 in** *Bibliography of Mauritius 1502-1954.*
Auguste Toussaint, H. Adolphe. Port Louis: Mauritius Archives, 1956. 884p.

Items 965-76 on p. 626-81 list the manuscripts at the Dutch Archives in The Hague (Bleyenburg 7) and the East India Company Archives in Amsterdam. These include ships' logs; papers relating to such subjects as the evacuation of Mauritius by the Dutch (1695-1706); and records concerning private trade in Mauritius; and the administration of Hubert Hugo (1673-77) and other Dutch governors.

Renseignements pour servir à l'histoire de l'Île Maurice. (Historical notes on Mauritius.)
See item no. 154.

The French period (1715-1810)

152 **Sea fights and corsairs of the Indian Ocean, being the naval history of Mauritius from 1715-1810.**
H.C.M. Austen. Port Louis: R.W. Brooks, Government Printer, 1935. 215p.

The French corsairs of the Indian Ocean not only provided a colourful story in their own right, but played an important part in the struggle between the European powers for trade routes, and subsequently in the aftermath of the French revolution and the British–French naval war. This book traces the history of the corsairs, and includes a useful section on the life of the famous French governor of the Ile de France, Mahé de La Bourdonnais.

153 **L'Ile Maurice et la révolution française.** (Mauritius and the French Revolution.)
Edited by Uttam Bissoondoyal, Asha L. Sibartie. Moka, Mauritius: Mahatma Gandhi Institute Press, 1990. 263p.

A collection of research papers presented at the conference held in August 1989 at the Mahatma Gandhi Institute in Mauritius to commemorate the bicentenary of the French Revolution (1789-1989) and Mauritius. The work of various scholars, the papers range from politics and constitution to literature; they highlight the political and philosophical ideas and ideologies of the 18th century – the age of 'rationalism' and the 'century of enlightenment' in France – and their impact on the Isle de France.

154 **Renseignements pour servir à l'histoire de l'Île Maurice.** (Historical notes on Mauritius.)
Adrien d'Epinay, Jr.   Mauritius: Nouvelle Imprimerie Dupuy, 1890.
601p.

The period covered in this detailed account includes the discovery of the island, the Dutch settlements, and French occupation up to 1810 when the British took over the administration. The d'Epinays were French 'colons'.

155 **The history of Mauritius or the Isle de France and the neighbouring islands: from their first discovery to the present time.**
Charles Grant, Viscount of Vaux.   London: W. Bulmer & Co., 1801.
571p. maps.

The author's objective in writing this book was to '[enlarge] the acquaintance of Great Britain and of the public in general with a very important part of the Eastern world' (sic). Written with the help of the papers and memoirs of Baron Grant, Charles Grant's father, who resided in the island for twenty years, the book begins with a geographical description of the Isle de France, followed by a section on natural history, then a chronological account of the officials appointed to the island's government from the time of the first colonial settlement to 1800. It describes the manners, customs and appearance of the inhabitants of Mauritius, other than the French settlers; lists the agricultural, marine and civil establishments under Mahé de La Bourdonnais; describes the island of Rodrigues; and examines the historical links between India and the Isle de France.

156 **France in the Indian Ocean.**
Jean Houbert.   Perth, Australia: University of Western Australia, Western Australian Institute of Technology, Western Australian College of Advanced Education and Murdoch University, 1984. 41p. bibliog.

This paper was produced for the second conference on Indian Ocean Studies at Perth, Western Australia. It focuses on the reasons for the development of Réunion as a *département* of France, and examines French policy in Mauritius, Rodrigues and the Comoros.

157 **Réunion island, French decolonization in the Mascareignes.**
Jean Houbert.   *Journal of Commonwealth and Comparative Politics*, vol. 18, no. 2 (1980), p. 145-71. bibliog.

This article attempts to explain the background to French policies of decolonization in Réunion by means of an historical review of the French presence in Mauritius and other islands. It also describes the conflict between UN resolutions concerning nationalism and sovereignty in the Indian Ocean and *de facto* French policy in islands such as Mauritius.

158 **In the grips of the Eagle.**
Huguette Ly Thio Fane. Moka, Mauritius: MGI Press, 1988. 223p.
maps.

This book provides an understanding of the conditions in the Isle de France under the last French governor Decaen (1803-10). A full and critical analysis is made of the circumstances of Matthew Flinders, a British prisoner, and useful appendices are included.

159 **Mauritius and the spice trade: the odyssey of Pierre Poivre.**
Edited by Madeleine Ly-Tio-Fane. Port Louis, Mauritius: Esclapon, 1958. 148p. bibliog. (Mauritius Archives Publication Fund Publication, no. 4).

An account of the French breakthrough in the 18th-century spice trade, which broke the Dutch monopoly of the time. It is told mainly through the life story of Pierre Poivre, a key figure in Mauritian history, and one of the most important and innovative French colonial administrators. The book explains why Mauritius did not become a major producer of spices, but remained as the main nursery and research station in the 19th century. It comprises forty-four documents, reproduced in French with English subtitles, and an introduction in English selected from the Mauritius Archives, the Mauritius Institute and the Archives Nationales, Paris. Madeleine Ly-Tio-Fane is a member of the Geographical and Historical Association of Mauritius, and Assistant Librarian at the Mauritius Institute.

160 **The triumph of Jean Nicolas Céré and his Isle Bourbon collaborators.**
Madeleine Ly-Tio-Fane. Paris: Mouton, 1968. 302p. bibliog.

A sequel to *Mauritius and the spice trade: the odyssey of Pierre Poivre* (q.v.) by the same author, this collection of documents continues the illustration of the story of the cultivation of spices in the islands of Mauritius (Isle de France) and Réunion (Bourbon) in the 18th century. The text is in English and French, with a clear and detailed introduction.

161 **L'esclavage à l'Isle de France de 1715 à 1810.** (Slavery in Mauritius 1715-1810.)
Karl Noël. France: Editions Two Cities, 1991. 190p. bibliog.

Based largely on contemporary accounts of slavery in Mauritius, the author argues that slaves in Mauritius were treated less harshly than those in the Caribbean. The book was originally a doctoral thesis submitted to the Sorbonne, and its conclusions will perhaps be challenged because of the paucity of available statistical information in support of the author's conclusions.

162 **Doléances des peuples coloniaux à l'assemblée coloniale constituante (1789-1790).** (Complaints of the inhabitants of the colonies at the colonial constituent assembly [1789-1790].)
Monique Pouliquen. Paris: Archives Nationales, 1989. 164p.

This is a study of the concerns of the settlers and free coloured people in Mauritius at the time of the French aspirations to a new society based on the Declaration of Human Rights in 1789. The Mauritian French settlers remain rigid, however, in their attitude to slavery. This illustrated book, written in French, is a collection of some twenty articles on the subject.

163 **L'Ile de France sous Decaen 1803-1810/essai sur la politique coloniale du premier Empire et la rivalité de la France et de l'Angleterre dans les Indes Orientales.** (Mauritius under Decaen 1803-10/essay on the colonial policy of the First Empire and the rivalry between France and England in the East Indies.)
Henri Prentout. Paris: Hachette, 1901. 688p. map.

A formidable 'essay' written in French with some *élan*, giving a detailed account of the Ile de France under the governorship of General Charles Decaen. It culminates in the capture of the island by the English forces in 1810, after which its name reverted to Mauritius. This detailed, colourful work emphasizes British and French political rivalry in the Indian Ocean, French diplomatic policy and the military outcome.

164 **L'administration française de l'Ile Maurice et ses archives (1721-1810).** (French administration of Mauritius and its archives [1721-1810].)
Auguste Toussaint. Port Louis: Government Printer, 1965. [n.p.]. bibliog. (Mauritius Archives Publications, no. 8).

An assemblage of factual information concerning the French colonial period, by Mauritius's indefatigable chief archivist. This volume covers details of the administration by departments, in chronological order, along with details of commissions dealing with social conditions. An introduction, tables and an index are included.

165 **Early American trade with Mauritius.**
Auguste Toussaint. Port Louis, Mauritius: Esclapon, 1954. 86p. (Mauritius Archives Publications).

A collection of annotated documents by Mauritius's former chief archivist, selected from archives in Mauritius and Washington DC, USA, covering the years 1793-1803. It is supplemented by a calendar of American voyages to the Isle de France from 1786 to 1810.

166 **Histoire politique de l'Isle de France.** (Political history of the Isle de France.)
Raymond d'Unienville. Port Louis: Mauritius Archives Publications, 1975 (vol. 1), 1982 (vol. 2). 191p.; 261p. bibliog.

This is a well-researched book, written in French, based on documentary evidence of primary sources. Volume 1 covers the years 1789-91, and Volume 2, 1791-94. The French Revolution was not confined to France; it had profound effects on the French colonial societies of the West Indies and the Mascarenes. The constitution changes effected in France with the creation of the National Assembly, a democratic institution, triggered off parallel changes in Isle de France (Mauritius). The colonists seized power and designed a constitution based on the principles of separation of powers and popular sovereignty. These scholarly books describe in detail the political and constitutional evolution from 1789 to 1794, and provide the basis for further research work in the field of history and constitution for the period 1787-94.

167 **Histoire politique de l'Isle de France 1795-1803.** (Political history of the
     Isle de France.)
     Raymond d'Unienville.   Port Louis: Mauritius Archives Publications,
     1989. 343p. 2 vols. bibliog.

Based on original documents, this book is a continuation of the author's study of the
1789-94 period. It describes the internal politics of the island; the colonial assemblies;
the parliament, its composition, functions and problems. All important events of the
period are related in detail, including how the island broke relations with France when
slavery was abolished. Relations were later re-established under Decaen, the last
French governor.

Voyage à l'Isle de France. (Voyage to the Isle de France.)
See item no. 89.

Voyage aux colonies orientales. (Voyage to the Eastern colonies.)
See item no. 90.

Journal historique fait au Cap de Bonne Espérance. (Historical journal
written at the Cape of Good Hope,)
See item no. 92.

Voyage dans les mers de l'Inde. (Voyage in the Indian seas.)
See item no. 102.

Ile Maurice, ancienne isle de France, fille de la révolution. (Mauritius, former
Isle de France, daughter of the revolution.)
See item no. 139.

La franc-maçonnerie à l'Ile Maurice. (Freemasonry in Mauritius.)
See item no. 420.

The British period (1810-1968)

168 **Charles Darwin and the Indian Ocean: archive use in the elucidation of
     an incident in the history of science.**
     Patrick Armstrong.   Perth, Australia: University of Western
     Australia, Western Australian Institute of Technology, Western
     Australian College of Advanced Education and Murdoch University,
     1984. 8p. maps. bibliog.

Patrick Armstrong here presents an essay from the second international conference on
Indian Ocean Studies at the University of Western Australia. He investigates the
sources that show to what extent Darwin's theories were affected by his travels in the
Indian Ocean.

169   **Blue book for the colony of Mauritius and its dependencies.**
Colony of Mauritius.   Port Louis: Government Printer, 1858-1938,
1945-47. annual.

A yearly review of all government activities in the British colony. Many volumes
include information on budgets, census reports and trade statistics. Slight variations in
the title occurred over the period of its publication.

170   **Les mauriciens dans la deuxième guerre mondiale.** (Mauritians in the
Second World War.)
F.R. Domingo.   Rose Hill, Mauritius: Editions de L'Océan Indien,
1983. 108p.

Many Mauritians fought, or were involved in, the war of 1939-45, when the country
was a British colonial possession. The author's intention is to show succeeding
generations of Mauritians the involvement of their ancestors in a conflict that was not
of their making.

171   **A great reformer: Sir Arthur Hamilton Gordon (1871-74).**
Marie Lise Frappier de Montbenoit.   [n.p.], 1986. 220p.

This is an MA dissertation on Hamilton Gordon, governor of Mauritius between 1871
and 1874, and his administration. The planters with whom he took issue over the
matter of Indian immigrant labourers made his life so difficult that he had to resign.
However, he succeeded in getting a Royal Commission to look into the living
conditions of the indentured cane workers.

172   **British Mauritius: 1810-1948.**
Dayachand Napal.   Port Louis: The Author, 1984. 256p. bibliog.

This book covers the island's history from the British conquest of the island to 1948,
when a new era of constitutional development began with the rise of 'nationalism'. On
British conquest, Isle de France became Mauritius, which was the name given it by the
Dutch settlers, but the lives of the inhabitants remained unchanged. Sir R.T. Farquhar
(1810-23) was the first British governor of the island.

173   **The history of slavery in Mauritius and the Seychelles, 1810-1875.**
Moses D.E. Nwulia.   Rutherford, New Jersey: Fairleigh Dickinson
University Press, 1981. 246p. maps. bibliog.

The heritage of slavery is a paramount factor in the make-up of Mauritius and
Seychelles. Its development is traced from the original black slaves brought by the
Dutch in the 17th century, through the years of French and English colonial rule.
There is an account of the post-emancipation period, and a conclusion which discusses
the effect of slavery on the islands' social hierarchy and the later exploitation of Indian
labour.

174   **Restless energy – a biography of Adolphe de Plevitz.**
Loretta de Plevitz.   Moka, Mauritius: Mahatma Gandhi Institute
Press, 1987. 251p. bibliog.

The book narrates the life-history of the German planter, Adolphe de Plevitz, who
settled in Mauritius in the mid-19th century and became a champion of Indian rights in

the colony. A popular figure among the sugar-cane workers, he was the force behind the setting-up of the Royal Commission to look into their treatment and living conditions. This finally led to amendments in the labour laws.

Descriptive account of Mauritius, its scenery, statistics, with a brief historical sketch preceded by elements of geography (the latter designed for youth).
See item no. 23.

Sub-tropical rambles in the land of the aphanapteryx.
See item no. 108.

Demographic survey of the British colonial empire.
See item no. 182.

The indenture system in Mauritius, 1837-1915.
See item no. 204.

A new system of slavery (The export of Indian labour overseas 1830-1920).
See item no. 208.

Approches de la pratique missionnaire catholique à l'Île Maurice entre 1840 et 1895. (Catholic missionaries in Mauritius, 1840-95.)
See item no. 228.

L'Eglise à Maurice 1810-1841. (The Church in Mauritius 1810-41.)
See item no. 233.

The revision movement (and the present state of political affairs in Mauritius).
See item no. 250.

L'Ile Maurice entre la France et l'Angleterre. (Mauritius between France and England.)
See item no. 251.

Modern Mauritius. The politics of decolonization.
See item no. 254.

L'Ile Maurice depuis sa conquête par l'Angleterre. (Mauritius since its conquest by the British.)
See item no. 363.

L'oeuvre du Révérend Jean Lebrun à l'Île Maurice. (The work of Reverend Jean Lebrun in Mauritius.)
See item no. 405.

Pre- and post-independence (1968-)

175 **Promises to keep.**
Uttam Bissoondoyal. Moka, Mauritius: Mahatma Gandhi Institute, 1989. 270p.

The story of the Bissoondoyal brothers and their political, cultural and religious movements. These were influenced by the struggle of Mahatma Gandhi, and looked forward to the eventual independence of Mauritius.

176 **Diego Garcia in international diplomacy.**
K.S. Jawatkar. New Delhi: Sangam Books, 1983. 360p. bibliog.

Dr. Jawatkar, an assistant professor in International Relations at Jawaharlal Nehru University, New Delhi, has written a detailed and well-argued study of the issue of Diego Garcia. The island was developed as a US military base against the wishes of most of the Indian Ocean territories. The book covers the history of the affair and international reaction to it, against the background of the Cold War. Diego Garcia was detached from Mauritius by the British colonial government in 1965, to constitute the British Indian Ocean Territory together with other islands. There are annexes on official documents, references and an index.

177 **Listwar lagrev ut 1979.** (An account of the August 1979 strike.)
Lalit. Port Louis: Ledikasyon Pu Travayer, 1986. 184p.

This is an historical account, in Creole, of an important event in post-independence Mauritius i.e., the nationwide general strike of August 1979 in support of claims associated with a referendum concerning the sugar industry. The referendum had been held in order to determine the official recognition of the Sugar Industry Labourer's Union.

178 **Mauritius in transition.**
Jay Narain Roy. Sammelan Mudranalaya, Allahabad, India: The Author, 1960. 502p.

Jay Narain Roy, a well-known Mauritian educator, writer, legislator and economist, covers the history, social and cultural climate and political prospects of his country at a time when it was beginning to work out its future as an independent nation. The book is very much a personal account, but is perceptive and of great value as a comment on the pre-independence period.

Mauritius. Democracy and development in the Indian Ocean.
See item no. 3.

The struggle of Dr. Ramgoolam.
See item no. 252.

Modern Mauritius. The politics of decolonization.
See item no. 254.

An act to serve. Sir Veerasamy Ringadoo.
See item no. 257.

La droit à l'excès. (The right to excess.)
See item no. 258.

Profiles of great Mauritians/Curé, Anquetil, Rozemont, Seeneevassen.
See item no. 265.

Population and Demography

General

179 **L'Ile Maurice et ses populations.** (Populations of Mauritius.)
Jean-Pierre, Joyce Durand.   Paris: Presses Universitaires de France,
1978. 188p. map. bibliog.
The authors examine the multicultural nature of Mauritian society against the historical
and economic background. They discuss the development of political change in the
1970s, mainly through the tenets of the emergent MMM (Mouvement Militant
Mauricien) party.

180 **Ile Maurice. Regulations des naissances et action familiale.** (Birth
control and family planning.)
François Guy, Michèle Guy.   Lyons, France: Editions Xavier Mappus,
1968. 342p. map.
The result of two years' work (1965-66) with the family planning organization in
Mauritius. The authors provide an introductory geographical and historical note, and
go on to trace the growth of the population in Mauritius. They discuss the formation of
the Mauritius Welfare Association in 1957 and the Action Familiale, the Roman
Catholic-backed family planning organization. The problems of religious groups, and
the social background and training of family planning educators are also covered.

181 **Mouvements de populations dans l'Océan Indien.** (Population
movements in the Indian Ocean.)
Indian Ocean International Historical Association.   Paris: Librairie H.
Champion, 1980. 459p. bibliog.
A collection of twenty-five papers in French and English which had its origin in a
meeting at Saint-Denis, Réunion, in 1972. 'Archival documentation on the Indian
emigration to Indian Ocean countries in the 19th century and 20th century', by D.G.

Keswani, is the most relevant to Mauritius, but there are a number of other papers of interest.

182 **Demographic survey of the British colonial empire.**
R.R. Kuczynski, Geoffrey Cumberlege.   Oxford: Oxford University Press, 1949. 2 vols. bibliog.

Issued in two volumes under the auspices of the Royal Institute of International Affairs, this useful study gives a detailed history of census-taking and other means of recording the number of people in the country (1753-1944). Volume 2 (p. 706-946) deals exclusively with Mauritius, its dependencies and the Seychelles. Rich with tables of statistics, it provides researchers with ample statistical data culled from official censuses and other records on immigration; emigration; births and deaths. Unfortunately, the book in Mauritius is only available in the Mauritius Archives.

183 **A comparative study of Mauritian immigrants in two European cities: London and Paris/an investigation into the problems of adaptation.**
Sam Lingayah.   London: The Author, 1991. 162p.

Lingayah is a field social worker for the London Borough of Hackney. This study covers the social problems faced by Mauritian immigrants, and attributes many of them to the legacy of colonialism. The author suggests that the immigrants' situation be re-evaluated if they are to 'survive and succeed'.

184 **Mauritian immigrants in Britain. A study of their hopes and frustrations.**
Sam Lingayah.   London: Mauritians' Welfare Association, 1987. 254p. bibliog.

Sociologist Lingayah's comprehensive study of Mauritian immigrants in Britain is written from a subjective and partly autobiographical viewpoint. The study includes many case histories. There is also an index.

Linguistic diversity and the quest for national identity: the case of Mauritius.
See item no. 214.

The physical quality of life in the Indian Ocean.
See item no. 237.

Fertility change in Mauritius and the impact of the family planning programme.
See item no. 246.

Women in Mauritius (in figures).
See item no. 473.

A plural society

185 **Vivre au pluriel.** (Living in the plural.)
Jean-Luc Albert, with the collaboration of Michael Watin.
La Réunion: University of Réunion, 1990. 183p.
A social study in identity of the populations of Mauritius and Réunion, whose history overlaps. Both islands had an influx of Indian labourers who came to work on the sugar plantations though the total numbers and proportions of immigrants involved in the two islands were different. This study, written in French, is available at the library of the School of Oriental and African Studies, University of London.

186 **Créoles, Indian immigrants and the restructuring of society and economy in Mauritius, 1767-1885.**
Richard Blair Allen.   University Microfilms International, 1987. 284p. map. bibliog.
In this thesis written for the University of Illinois in 1983, Allen argues that not enough account has been taken of Mauritius's important role in the history of European colonialism, the slave trade, immigration from the Indian sub-continent and the development of pluralistic societies during the 19th and early 20th centuries. Researched in Mauritius and Europe, the book is a readable, as well as scholarly, study of these themes. There is a glossary and notes on sources and documents.

187 **The Afro-Mauritians. An essay.**
Gaëtan Benoît.   Moka, Mauritius: Mahatma Gandhi Institute Press, 1985. 105p.
A study of the contribution made by the Mauritians descended from Africans to Mauritius's pluralistic society. The book covers, briefly, the history, culture and social development of the Afro-Mauritians from the first Dutch importation of slaves to Mauritius in the 17th century. This was followed by a rise in the numbers under French and British rule. It also discusses the contribution of the Afro-Mauritians to the culture of contemporary Mauritian society. There are some illustrations. This is a scholarly work, but of general interest.

188 **The population of Mauritius – fact, problem and policy.**
S. Chandrasekhar.   New Delhi: Indus Publishing, 1990. 90p. bibliog.
This is an interesting work, though brief, by an Indian demographer who edits *Population Review*, a journal of demography of the developing countries. After outlining the history of population in Mauritius from 1500 to 1985, Chandrasekhar delves with more detail into the period 1834 to 1910 which coincides with (immigrant) labour importation from India. The book analyses the factors that make Mauritius a plural society, with the special problems that this poses, and the consideration of local situations that any social policy entails in view of its population charactersitics. The third chapter makes special reference to Indian immigration to Mauritius and the island's population problem. There are bibliographical notes to each chapter with several statistical tables on population growth, distribution and composition. This forms a good basis for further research in the field.

189   **The Muslims in Mauritius.**
      Moomtaz Emrith.   Goodlands, Mauritius: Regent Press, 1966. 172p.
An account of the history of Muslim immigration and settlement in Mauritius from
1722, with chapters on the social and political development of the Muslim community
in the 1960s. It is illustrated with an appendix of extracts from the Memorandum of the
Muslim Community of 1932 to the Secretary of State for the Colonies. A further
account of the Moslem community can be found in Raymond Delval's 'La communauté
musulmane de l'Ile Maurice' ('The Mauritian Moslem community') and in 'Aspects de
l'Islam contemporain dans l'Ocean Indien' ('Some aspects of contemporary Islam in
the Indian Ocean'), *Annuaire des pays de l'Océan Indien*, vol. 6, 1979.

190   **L'Ile Maurice. (Mauritius.)**
      Bernard Lehembre.   Paris: Editions Karthala, 1984. 244p.
This illustrated book, written in French, describes the successive waves of immigration
to Mauritius in the 18th and 19th centuries, and shows how the expansion of the sugar-
cane plantations created the demand for immigrant workers from India. It goes on to
show how the present multiracial population of Mauritius developed.

191   **Chinese diaspora in Western Indian Ocean.**
      Huguette Ly-Tio-Fane Pineo.   Stanley, Rose-Hill, Mauritius: Editions
      de l'Océan Indien/Chinese Catholic Mission, 1985. 424p. maps. bibliog.
A study of the Chinese minorities settled in the Western Indian Ocean, set against a
historical and social background. Reference is made to the colonial rivalries in the
Indian Ocean territories and the developing island states. The book also traces the
decline of imperial China, which enabled its citizens to emigrate to new lands overseas,
including Mauritius. The French edition (*Diaspora chinoise dans l'Océan Indien
occidental*) was published in 1981 by Presses G.I.S. Méditerranée, Aix-en-Provence,
France. The English edition contains some illustrations.

Mauritius/The problems of a plural society.
See item no. 1.

Mauritius: the development of a plural society.
See item no. 14.

Indians in a plural society: a report on Mauritius.
See item no. 195.

Rise and fall of three leaders/Bissoondoyal, Mohamed, Koenig.
See item no. 266.

History of Indian immigration

192 Tamils in Mauritius.
T. Ammigan.   Ste. Croix, Mauritius: Proag Printing, 1989. 48p.

The author, who has studied Tamil culture at the Tamil University of Tarjavur, India, surveys the history and present position of the Mauritian Tamil community. The book covers all aspects of the community, including social, cultural and economic affairs.

193 Annual report on free passages granted to return immigrants.
Mauritius Archives.   Port Louis: Government Printer, 1880-85.

This report contains an account of the working of the immigration department; detailed statistics of the repatriation of immigrants on account of disease, by order of protector or government; detailed list of names, immigrant numbers and districts; the return to India; and the reasons for granting free return passages.

194 Les indiens à l'Ile Maurice. (Indians in Mauritius.)
Anauth Beejadhur.   Port Louis: La Typographie Moderne, 1935. 124p.

This book was written by a well-known figure in modern Mauritian politics, Beejadhur (1909-81), who was a minister as well as a journalist. He considers the history of the Indian immigrant cane workers who settled in Mauritius, and the position they held in Mauritian society at that time. There is a useful appendix of arrivals and departures of the Indian immigrants.

195 Indians in a plural society: a report on Mauritius.
Burton Benedict.   London: HMSO, 1961. 170p. maps. bibliog. (Colonial Research Study, no. 34).

This book is a detailed account of the history, role and organization of the various groups of Indian origin in Mauritian society. The study shows the importance of the diverse Asian community, which formed two-thirds of Mauritian population at the time the book was written. The author traces the elements of conflict as well as solidarity among Hindus and Muslims and presages, in the final chapter, the later political development of Mauritius.

196 Indian labour immigration.
Edited by Uttam Bissoondoyal.   Moka, Mauritius: Mahatma Gandhi Institute Press, 1986. 328p. bibliog.

This is an important contribution to any study on the subject of Indian labour immigration. It comprises a collection of papers presented on the occasion of the 150th anniversary of Indian immigration in 1984, and includes tables, bibliographical notes, statistics on indentured labourers and some illustrations.

197 **Indians overseas/The Mauritian experience.**
Edited by Uttam Bissoondoyal. Moka, Mauritius: Mahatma Gandhi
Institute, 1984. 438p. bibliog.
These scholarly articles build a comprehensive picture of subjects ranging from
'Indians and politics' to 'Indian convicts in Mauritius 1816-1953'. Many aspects of
Indian immigration to Mauritius are covered, from their cultural traditions to their
changing image in society, and their emerging political and economic role. Each paper
has its own selective bibliography. This is an important work for any student of the
history of Mauritius's population of Indian origin.

198 **Correspondence relating to Indian immigration.**
Mauritius Archives, 1859-1913.
A sample of the correspondence and a report relating to Indian immigration and
immigrants that can be consulted at the Folk Museum of Indian Immigration, Moka,
Mauritius. The letters comprise: 'Correspondence relating to the statements made in
the Council of Government on 15 November 1867 by Mr W.W.R. Kew, treasurer,
regarding the treatment of Indian immigrants in 1867-68'; 'Correspondence relating to
the condition of Indian immigrants in 1871'; 'Correspondence respecting the
introduction of the immigrant De Conray and his return to India in 1885';
'Correspondence on the high death-rate on sugar estates in 1906-07'; 'Correspondence
on the subject of the reorganization of the immigration & poor law departments in
1913'. The report is on the death rate on sugar estates for the last four years, the first
half being written by John Bolton. Collectively, they give a clear insight into the
conditions pertaining at the time.

199 **Report of Her Majesty's Royal Commissioners appointed to enquire into
the treatment/condition of Indian immigrants in Mauritius. Presented to
both Houses of Parliament by command of Her Majesty, 6th Feb. 1875
(C-115).**
W.E. Frere, V.A. Williamson. London: William Clowes & Sons,
1875.
The commission was appointed in 1872, following complaints about the living
conditions of the labourers brought in from India to work on the sugar estates. The
findings of the commission led to the 1878 Labour Laws which gave the Indian workers
greater protection. Some of the evidence given before the Royal Commission of
enquiry into the condition and treatment of Indian immigrants in Mauritius is recorded
in W.J. Day and W.C. Connor's publication by J. Lafitte's Stream Printing
Establishment in 1873.

200 **History of Indians in Mauritius.**
K. Hazareesingh. London; Basingstoke, England: Macmillan
Education Ltd., 1977. 157p. bibliog.
This volume is primarily a history of the Indian labourers in Mauritius covering social,
cultural, economic and political developments. It represents a significant contribution
to historical research on Indian immigration to, and human settlements on, the island.
The first Indian immigrants came to Mauritius in 1736, when the island was a French
colony, having been recruited from Pondicherry by La Bourdonnais, then Governor of
Mauritius. However, they came in significant numbers after the abolition of slavery, by

which time the island had passed on to British control, to work mainly on the sugar estates and to become an ethnic and cultural majority.

201 **Les Indiens à l'Isle de France.** (Indians in the Isle de France.)
Doojendranath Napal.   Port Louis: Editions Nationales, 1965. 74p.

The author gives a brief account of Indian immigration to Mauritius in the 18th century during French occupation of the island, prior to mass immigration from the year 1834. The first Indians came from Bourbon (Réunion) and accompanied the first French colonists to the Isle de France and were 'slaves'. In 1729, thirteen slaves from Bengal and a hundred boys and girls from the Coromandel Coast of India were brought to Mauritius to work as servants. Later the French governor, Mahé de La Bourdonnais imported more Indian labour from Pondicherry; these were mainly artisans who built the capital Port Louis. Other groups arrived, and the author quotes documents to support his findings. There is no bibliography.

202 **Précis showing the different phases through which immigration to Mauritius from the East Indies had passed before it assumed its present form.**
Léon Koenig.   Port Louis: Government Printers, 1905. 71p.

This study was prepared for a commission appointed by his Excellency the governor on 21 Jan. 1905, set up to inquire into a report on the question of reducing the cost of the introduction of Indian immigrants into Mauritius. It was also to address itself to general questions concerning emigration and immigration relating to Mauritius.

203 **Lettre du conseil supérieur de l'Ile de France (16 mai 1769).** (Letter of 16 May 1769 of the Superior Council of the Ile de France.)
Archives de Pondicherry.   [n.p.], 1730-1815.

This letter relates to Indian emigration to Mauritius, and dates back to the time when Mauritius was a French colony. The Pondicherry records include letters by various persons to the Isle de France, a large number of which relate to Indian emigration and are of Mauritian interest.

204 **The indenture system in Mauritius, 1837-1915.**
S.B. Mookerji.   Calcutta: Firma K.L. Mukhopodhyay, 1962. 66p.

Mookerji relates the history of Indian immigration during its peak period and explains the indenture system of labour. More than 400,000 Indian labourers came to Mauritius with half that number recruited between 1837 and 1870. This influx of immigrants was to change the composition of the Mauritian population for the Indians became the ethnic majority.

205 **P.A. protectorate of immigrants: 1-296.**
Port Louis: Mauritius Archives, [n.d.].

Bound copies of the letters received by the protector of immigrants from the Mauritius emigration agencies in India, from the secretariat and other departments, and from various persons (1844-1909). Copies of the letters (outletters 1-54) sent by the protector of immigrants from 1843 to 1911 are also available.

206   **Les Tamouls à l'Ile Maurice.** (The Tamils in Mauritius.)
      Ramoo Sooriamoorthy.   Les Pailles, Mauritius: Henry & Co. Ltd.,
      1977. 244p. bibliog.
Written in French, the book relates the history of Mauritians of South Indian origin
whose forefathers came from the Madras Presidency as traders, artisans or labourers;
these were among the first to arrive on the island, from the time when the country was
under French rule. Biographical details of the island's well-known 'tamouls' are given,
tracing their achievements to their origins. These achievements are a source of great
pride to the author. There are a number of photographs included.

207   **Indians overseas: a guide to source materials in the India Office Records
      for the study of Indian migration, 1830-1950.**
      Timothy N. Thomas.   London: British Library, 1985. 112p.
A valuable introduction to the documentation held at the India Office of Records
relating to the migration of Indian citizens to other parts of the Commonwealth and
elsewhere between 1830 and 1950.

208   **A new system of slavery (The export of Indian labour overseas 1830-
      1920).**
      Hugh Tinker.   London: Oxford University Press for the Institute of
      Race Relations, 1974. 441p. maps. bibliog.
This is a history of Indian immigrants in the British colonies in the 19th century. It
studies the entire process of emigration from rural India, across the ocean in
overcrowded ships to some ten different colonies including Mauritius, where they
expected a better life. There are eighteen black-and-white photographs, two diagrams
and an index.

209   **Reports of the protector of immigrants.**
      J.F. Trotter. [n.p.], 1882, 1883, 1884 and 1889.
The above reports have been included here to guide further research into Indian
immigration in Mauritius. Many such others are available at the Folk Museum of
Indian Immigration, Mahatma Gandhi Institute, in Moka. The first concerns 're-
engagement of Indian labourers on sugar estates and re-opening of immigration from
India'; the second relates to 'vagrancy amongst the Indian population'; the 1883 paper
reports on the 'non-compliance with requisitions for Indian labourers'; 1884 is the 'final
report of the special commissioner appointed to enquire into the working of the
emigration agencies of Mauritius in Madras & Calcutta'; and 1889 reports on the
'recruiting operation'.

Restless energy – a biography of Adolphe de Plevitz.
See item no. 174.

**The religion and culture of Indian immigrants in Mauritius and the effect of
social change.**
See item no. 231.

Population and Demography. History of Indian immigration

The Indian Christian community in Mauritius.
See item no. 234.

Namasté. (Greetings.)
See item no. 436.

Languages

General

210 **Ile Maurice: une francophonie paradoxale.** (Mauritius: A paradox of French inheritance.)
Daniel Baggioni, Didier de Robillard.   Paris: L'Harmattan, 1990. 185p. bibliog.
A study of the French language legacy in Mauritius, more than 250 years since it was brought to the island by the French settlers. The socio-linguistic context is examined together with the related pedagogical problems. Various diagrams illustrate the text.

211 **Hindi in Mauritius.**
Somdath Buckory.   Stanley, Rose Hill, Mauritius; Editions de l'Océan Indien, 1988. 2nd ed. 137p.
This is a useful book for the Mauritian student of Hindi from a historical perspective (a language which used to be the mother tongue of more than half the population). First published in 1967, the book now contains a new chapter covering the years 1968 (when Mauritius attained independence) to 1988. It emphasizes the efforts that have been made during that time to enhance the Hindi language and other oriental languages, and also studies the development of the language over the years.

212 **Le parler franco-mauricien au Natal.** (Franco-Mauritian speech in Natal.)
Antoine J. Bullier.   Paris: Editions L'Harmattan, 1981. 182p. bibliog.
This book is based on a socio-linguistic survey of the speech of thirty-one Mauritians living in Natal, South Africa. It proceeds to analyse the various phonological elements in the French spoken by Mauritians (a phonological table is included). The author makes recommendations for the conservation of the language in the Natal community concerned.

213 **Bhojpuri and Creole in Mauritius.**
Nicole Z. Domingue. Austin, Texas: University of Texas, 1975.
[n.p.].
A study of linguistic interrelations and their consequences in language development. It is a PhD thesis and a copy is available in the School of Oriental and African Studies Library, University of London.

214 **Linguistic diversity and the quest for national identity: the case of Mauritius.**
Thomas Hylland Eriksen. *Ethnic and Racial Studies*, vol. 13, no. 1 (1990).
This essay describes the language situation in relation to nationalism and ethnicity as rival ideologies in Mauritian society. The political situation is assessed through the use of language and language policies on ethnic relations. It discusses the potential use of Creole as a national language and as a medium for the promotion of ethnic cooperation and nationalist ideology.

215 **Proposals for a rational language policy for the development of an integrated Mauritian personality.**
Ramesh Ramdoyal. Moka, Mauritius: Mauritius Institute of Education, 1982. 10p.
Ramdoyal points out the need for a language policy for the development of a solid Mauritian culture.

216 **Language teaching in the Indian Ocean.**
E. B. Richmond. New York, London: University Press of America, 1983. 48p. map.
This book studies three developing nations, Mauritius, Seychelles and Comoros in the context of national language policy and pedagogy. The research was done in 1982. Mauritius is dealt with in detail in chapter 2, p. 9-23. The author concludes that English has remained the official language in Mauritius 'more by default than by choice because of the cultural factions'.

The Mauritian kaleidoscope. Languages and religions.
See item no. 416.

Creole

217 **The contribution of non-francophone immigrants to the lexicon of Mauritian Creole.**
Philip Baker.   PhD thesis, School of Oriental and African Studies, University of London, 1982. 896p.

Baker's PhD thesis is a valuable contribution to the study of the role of other languages spoken in Mauritius to Creole's development and vocabulary.

218 **Etude sur le patois créole mauricien.** (A study of Mauritian Creole.)
Charles Baissac.   Nancy, France: Berger Levrault, 1880. 234p.

One of the first comprehensive studies of the Creole language of Mauritius, which has its roots in French, more than half a century after the British conquest of the island. Baissac also wrote about Creole tales and published a book about Mauritian folklore in Creole (q.v.).

219 **Le patois créole.** (Creole.)
Berthe du Pavillon.   Rose Hill, Mauritius: Editions de l'Océan Indien, 1988. 50p.

Originally part of a thesis written by Charles Baissac in 1880, this small book traces the origins of the Mauritian Creole language of that period, and gives French equivalents. The author's original spelling has been retained.

Archipel de Chagos en mission. (Chagos Archipelago: on a mission.)
See item no. 96.

Listwar lagrev ut 1979. (An account of the August 1979 strike.)
See item no. 177.

Dictionaries and grammar

220 **Dictionary of Mauritian Creole.**
Philip Baker, Vinesh Y. Hookoomsing.   Paris: L'Harmattan, 1987. 365p.

A comprehensive dictionary of Mauritian Creole with translations in English and French. The authors have included Creole words in current use, as well as those to be found in old texts. The research for this work began in 1967.

Languages. Dictionaries and grammar

221 **Parlez créole – Guide pratique pour touristes.** (Speak Creole – a tourist guide.)
James Burty David, Lilette David, Clarel Seenyen. Rose Hill, Mauritius: Editions de l'Océan Indien, 1988. 118p.

This is a practical guide for the English- or French-speaking visitor to Mauritius. The pronunciation of the Creole equivalent is based on the phonetics of the French or English language. There are stock phrases and sentences, useful in banks, markets and shops, and covering the needs of the tourist generally.

222 **Diksyoner Kreol-Angle: Diksyoner prototip Kreol-Angle.** (Creole-English dictionary.)
Ledikasyon pu Travayer. Port Louis: The Author, 1985. 250p.

This dictionary provides English translations of Creole. The Creole entries, with an emphasis on currently-used words and expressions, are written phonetically. The work is of considerable lexicographical interest. In the introduction to Baker's and Hookoomsing's dictionary (q.v.), it is stated that the first draft of *Diksyoner kreol morisyen* 'was used in the preparation of this dictionary'.

223 **How to write Kreol properly.**
Ledikasyon pu Travayer. Grand River Northwest, Port Louis: Ledikasyon pu Travayer, 1989. 54p.

Ledikasyon pu Travayer, a workers' association, produced this small booklet, less than pocket-sized, to help adults already literate in English and French to read and write Creole. It was produced partly to counteract the dissemination of the French language under an alleged French imperialist strategy of *francophonie*.

Religion

224 Les pratiques, rites et croyances de la religion populaire chinoise. 25 ans de la mission catholique chinoise à l'Ile Maurice. (The popular religious practice, rites and beliefs of the Chinese. 25 years of the Chinese Catholic mission in Mauritius.)
La mission catholique chinoise de l'Ile Maurice.   Port Louis: The Author, 1975. 56p.

The book discusses the different Chinese religious sects that thrive in the multicultural environment of Mauritius – namely Confucianism, Taoism and Buddhism. Written in French, the book describes Chinese–Mauritian religious practices, festivals, temples and culture and concludes with the evolution of the Chinese community in Mauritius.

225 Le mouvement Ahmadiyya dans l'Islam. (The Ahmadiyya Movement in Islam.)
H.M. Bashir-ud-Din Mahmud Ahmad, Khalifalul Masih II.   Port Louis: Ahmadiyya Association of Mauritius, 1964. 84p.

This is a comprehensive account of the Ahmadiyya movement in Mauritius. It outlines the history of the movement from its origin and theorizes on its relevance to Islam and the Holy Koran.

226 Deux indiens illustres – Dayananda et Gandhi. (Two famous Indians – Dayananda and Gandhi.)
B. Bissoondoyal.   Paris: Adyar, 1968. 96p.

The book relates the life history of two men whose philosophy influenced the course of Hinduism in Mauritius. Swami Dayananda never left India, while Gandhi visited Mauritius briefly. Founder of the Arya Samaj (Société des Hommes Nobles) in 1975, Dayananda (1824-83) founded his doctrine on the principle of egality of souls and universal brotherhood. A neo-Hindu movement, it is important in the development of contemporary religious practice of the Hindus on the island; it is against the caste system, child marriages and other similar practices. Gandhi's visit to Mauritius in 1901 gave a boost to the Hindu community on the island. There is an index of names.

227 What's wrong with the Hindus?
Sarita Boodhoo. Port Louis: Deen Bandhu Publications, 1981. 10p.

This is an attempt to raise Hindu consciousness among the Mauritian population and warn the Hindu community against loss of identity, in the context of what was seen as a campaign to sap Hindu unity and solidarity.

228 Approches de la pratique missionnaire catholique à l'Île Maurice entre 1840 et 1895. (Catholic missionaries in Mauritius, 1840-95.)
Didier Colson. Toulouse, France: University of Toulouse, 1980. 800p. bibliog.

This study of the operational methods of the Catholic missionaries in Mauritius covers a period when the island was under British rule (see Nagapen's study [q.v.]). It was submitted as a thesis for a PhD in theology. A copy is available at the University of Mauritius.

229 Evangil selon Sén Luk (dans langaz créole Maurice). (The gospel according to St. Luke in Mauritian Creole.)
James Forester Anderson. London: British & Foreign Bible Society, 1893. 90p.

Anderson also translated the three other gospels into Creole: St. Mark (1893, 50p); St. John (1896, 72p); and St. Matthew (1983, 80p). Later he went on to write a brief history of Protestantism, which was published in Paris in 1903, entitled *Esquisse de l'histoire du protestantisme à l'Ile Maurice et aux Iles Mascareignes* ('A brief history of Protestantism in Mauritius and the Mascarenes').

230 L'Islam à Maurice.
R.N. Gassita. Paris: Ernest Leroux, 1913. 44p. map.

This is a well-researched work on the ethnic origin and evolution of the Muslim community in Mauritius. It gives details of their geographical distribution and settlement, their religion, economic and educational achievements, political status, festivals and culture. There are twelve photographs of mosques and people.

231 The religion and culture of Indian immigrants in Mauritius and the effect of social change.
K. Hazareesingh. Port Louis: Indian Cultural Association, 1966.

This is an article that appeared in the *Indian Cultural Review* of July 1966, on the occasion of its 30th anniversary. It gives a brief survey of the Indian community and the impact of social change on their life and development prior to independence. The magazine appeared irregularly between 1936 and 1980; copies are available at the Mauritius Archives.

232 **Mauritius Legislative Council report.**
Port Louis, Mauritius: Government Printer, 1956. 17p. (Sessional Paper, no. 9 [1956]).

The report of the Commission appointed to examine the possibility of subsidizing religions not already receiving aid at the time in Mauritius.

233 **L'Eglise à Maurice 1810-1841.** (The Church in Mauritius 1810-41.)
Amédée Nagapen. Port Louis: Port Louis Diocese, 1984. 453p. bibliog.

This is a major piece of research work, written in French, by Father Nagapen. The book is an account of the emergence and role of the Catholic and Anglican churches in Mauritius during the first three decades of British rule. He gives details of the part played by missionaries in theological training and general education, with the creation of schools and the reaction of the existing French religious institutions. He discusses the interplay of religion and politics, the influence of religion on politics and government, and evangelization and anglicanization as a means of colonization. The book contains forty-four black-and-white illustrations. Trevor Huddleston's study on 'The role of the Anglican Church in Mauritius in the 1980s' completes the picture.

234 **The Indian Christian community in Mauritius.**
Amédée Nagapen. Port Louis: Roman Catholic Diocese of Port Louis/Mahatma Gandhi Institute, 1984. 25p. bibliog.

This book is based on original documents and traces the history and evolution of the Indian Christian community in the island, going back to 1722. Details are given of the evangelization of immigrants to Catholicism and Protestantism.

Promises to keep.
See item no. 175.

The Muslims in Mauritius.
See item no. 189.

La Vie Catholique. (Catholic Life.)
See item no. 483.

Social Conditions and Health

235 **Medical and sanitary matters in Mauritius.**
Andrew Balfour.   London: Waterlow & Sons Ltd., 1922. 168p. maps.
This is an illustrated report by Dr. Balfour which brings together several reports on the sanitary situation in various districts of the island. It highlights the prevailing medical conditions resulting from poor sanitation.

236 **Inégalité devant la mort.** (Inequality in death.)
J.S. Baligadoo.   Rose Hill, Mauritius: Editions de l'Océan Indien; Paris: SFERAMIS, 1986. 138p.
Professor Baligadoo discusses the problems of access, or the lack of it, to a doctor for Mauritians. He goes on to describe the problems of heart disease in the country, following research in a number of villages and urban centres. He compares the attitude to health in rich and poor countries and asks for more importance to be accorded to health in the latter.

237 **The physical quality of life in the Indian Ocean.**
Bruce E. Davis.   In: *ICIOS II. Second International Conference on Indian Ocean Studies at Perth Western Australia, 5-12 December 1984, Section A, Resources, Environment and Economic Development.*
Published through the cooperation of the University of Western Australia, Western Australian Institute of Technology, the Western Australian College of Advanced Education and Murdoch University, 1984. 6p. map. bibliog.
A statistical survey of the Indian Ocean islands' physical quality of life, based on data about infant mortality, life expectancy after the age of one and literacy after the age of fifteen. Mauritius ranks after Réunion in this survey. There is a population chart of the region.

238 Elle Maurice.

M. Dinan (et al.).   Mauritius: Soroptimist International – IPSAE,
1989. 85p.

This is a study of the situation of women in Mauritius presented through a collection of articles. It describes the woman's place in an insular society and attempts to foresee her future rule.

239 Report on the government orphan asylum at Powder Mills.

Thomas Elliott, A. Chasteauneuf.   Port Louis: Government Printer,
1875. 39p.

A commissioned report on the asylum for the Immigration Department undertaken in the context of the Royal Commission of 1872, which was appointed to look into allegations of ill-treatment of Indian labourers on the sugar estates.

240 Elle Rodrigues.

M.C. Luchman, M. Maurel.   Mauritius: Soroptimist International –
IPSAE, 1989. 85p.

A portrait of the life of the women of Rodrigues, set in the geographic, historical and social context of the second island of Mauritius. The book is based on interviews with the women of Rodrigues and analyses their joys, sorrows, hopes and despairs.

241 Social development in Mauritius. A study in rural modernization in an island community.

Shiv Rattan Mehta.   New Delhi: Wiley Eastern, 1981. 175p. bibliog.

Mehta presents the results of a sample survey on cultural and ethnic differences carried out in twenty-nine village council areas, and attempts to shed light on the potential for social development. The survey provides information on the value systems of the people, their reactions to development activities, political knowledge and aspirations for their children.

242 Guide pour la femme mauricienne. (Guide for the Mauritian woman.)

Ministry of Labour and Industrial Relations, Women's Rights and
Family Welfare.   Port Louis: The Ministry, [n.d.], 32p.

In French, this is a question-and-answer booklet giving practical advice on subjects from contraception and hygiene to government services and women's rights in law. It is simply and effectively written.

243 The women's liberation movement in Mauritius.

Muvman Liberasyon Fam.   Grand River Northwest, Port Louis:
Ledikasyon pu Travayer, 1988. 112p. maps.

Largely an account in English by the Muvman Liberasyon Fam (Women's Liberation Movement) of Mauritius's origins and subsequent history in the context of women's rights. It gives a comprehensive account of the background of women's problems in marriage, legal rights and cultural dynamic.

Social Conditions and Health

244 **Les mariées de l'Ile Maurice.** (Brides from Mauritius.)
Martyne Perrot. Paris: Bernard Grasset, 1983. 266p.

The author describes the lives of some of the Mauritian women who married Frenchmen and settled in France. The intent is sociological and the book is based on actual case histories, although names have been changed.

245 **Social policies and population growth in Mauritius. Report to the governor of Mauritius.**
Richard Titmuss, Brian Abel-Smith, assisted by Tony Lynes. London: Mathuew, 1961. 307p. (Sessional Paper No. 6, 1960).

A substantive report on the provisions to be made for social security in Mauritius, based on local studies made by the authors in 1959. There is an index together with tables, appendices and diagrams.

246 **Fertility change in Mauritius and the impact of the family planning programme.**
Christos Xenos. Mauritius: Ministry of Health, 1977. 426p. map. bibliog.

Resulting from a study in Mauritius to establish and head a Population Control Evaluation Programme, this very detailed and substantial work covers the whole range of population growth and family planning against the demographic and socio-economic setting of the country. It is a useful book for its analysis of a country which has considerable success in controlling the rise of its population. There are graphs, tables and appendices.

The economic and social structure of Mauritius. Report to the governor of Mauritius.
See item no. 17.

Politics

General

247 **Security and nationalism in the Indian Ocean: lessons from Latin Quarter islands.**
Philip M. Allen.   Boulder, Colorado: Westview Press, 1987. 260p. maps. bibliog.
Mauritius is among the five island nations covered in an analysis of their security, politics and peoples, and power bases. The UN resolutions declaring the Indian Ocean a zone of peace are covered in appendices.

248 **The Indian Ocean in global politics.**
Edited by Larry W. Bowman, Ian Clark.   Boulder, Colorado: Westview Press; Nedlands, Western Australia: University of Western Australia Press; New Delhi: Young Asia Publications, 1981. 251p. map. bibliog.
This is a collection of twelve papers presented at the International Conference on Indian Ocean Studies held at Perth, Australia, in August 1979. The military agreements between USA and Britain are discussed and are of particular importance to post-independence politics in Mauritius. An index completes the report.

249 **L'évolution nationale mauricienne.** (The Mauritian national evolution.)
J.A. Duclos.   Paris: Editions Jonne, 1924. 586p.
In French, the book traces the history of the retrocession movement, which started in 1919 as a reaction to a perceived collaboration between Britain and the Indo–Mauritian majority, and advocated a return of the island to France. This became the main issue of the 1921 elections. The majority proved to be against the movement, however. Duclos argues against retrocession and urges Mauritians to work for unity.

250 **The revision movement (and the present state of political affairs in Mauritius).**
A.F. Fokeer.   Rose Hill, Mauritius: Shiva Mayam Printing Establishment, 1927. 116p.

This book traces the history of the coloured population of Mauritius, their origins, their struggle for emancipation and their dissatisfaction with the policy of the British Colonial Government. It also outlines the main features of the retrocession movement and its failure. The defeat of the retrocession movement was succeeded by the revision movement, i.e. the revision of the Constitution, and several draft proposals were made. Indo–Mauritians were excluded from the Committee, and its failure is attributed to their non-collaboration. This is an informative and readable book, which gives a true picture of society and events in the 1920s. It is of considerable use to students of history and constitution, as several plans for constitutional change were proposed.

251 **L'Ile Maurice entre la France et l'Angleterre.** (Mauritius between France and England.)
Edouard Laurent.   Port Louis: Imprimerie de la Patrie, 1914. 2nd ed. 59p.

This work demands the retrocession of Mauritius to France as the British Government had failed to fulfil its promise to respect the terms of the Act of Capitulation of 1810. It accuses the British Government of despotism, red-tapeism and favouritism, and deplores the policy of concentrating all powers – legislative, executive and judicial – in the hands of the Governor. It claims political liberation for the coloured, and says that if Britain was unwilling to grant this, the island should be restored to France. This is a serious book for historians, politicians and students, but the general reader will also find it of interest. It is available at the Mauritius Archives.

252 **The struggle of Dr. Ramgoolam.**
Monindra Nath Varma.   Quatre Bornes, Mauritius: The Author, 1975. 236p.

This was written when Sir Seewoosagur Ramgoolam, the chief figure in Mauritian national politics for many years and the country's first Prime Minister, was seventy-five years old. The biography is uncritical, but provides a wealth of useful information on Mauritian politics in the years preceding independence.

253 **The African political dictionary.**
Claude S. Phillips.   Santa Barbara, California: ABC-Clio Information Services, 1984. 245p. maps. bibliog.

Mauritius is included in the Anglophone African section of this dictionary, which provides basic information about African politics. The chapters deal with subjects such as land and peoples, resistance to colonialism, and political culture and ideology, with the key themes listed alphabetically. Mauritius's constitutional development, language policies and external relations are covered.

254 **Modern Mauritius. The politics of decolonization.**
Adele Smith Simmons, foreword by Gwendolen M. Carter.
Bloomington, Indiana: Indiana University Press, 1982. 242p. map.
bibliog.

Simmons examines the political development of Mauritius from a British colonial possession to independence in 1968. This book is written primarily for a US undergraduate readership, and sets out to analyse the process by which a multi-ethnic island society started to organize itself politically, and take a largely non-violent, but never straightforward, path to independence. The strategic importance of Mauritius in modern history is underlined and the book sketches in the early history of Mauritius, tracing the various political movements back to their beginnings.

Mauritius: the development of a plural society.
See item no. 14.

The women's liberation movement in Mauritius.
See item no. 243.

Pre- and post-independence

255 **Gandhi and Mauritius and other essays.**
Uttam Bissoondoyal.   Moka, Mauritius: Mahatma Gandhi Institute
Press, 1988. 149p.

A collection of occasional articles which have appeared in newspapers, together with some speeches and lectures of Uttam Bissoondoyal. They are based on the visit of Mahatma Gandhi to Mauritius in 1901, and its impact on the island's political thinking.

256 **Pour l'autonomie.** (For autonomy.)
Anatole de Bourcherville.   Port Louis: Imprimerie de La Patrie, 1914.
141p.

This informative, analytical work refutes the chapter entitled 'La politique et la population' which Hon Léclezio presented to Macmillan for publication in his book *Mauritius illustrated*, and in which Léclezio praised the British Colonial Government. Bourcherville criticizes the oligarch's attitude of servile conformity to the British Colonial Government and politics merely for economic advantages. In the same breath Bourcherville, one of the founders of Action Libérale (the earliest political party at the turn of 20th century), demands self-government for Mauritius and a share for other ethnic groups (mainly for the coloured) in the political life of the island. The book will be of interest to historians and students of government politics and constitutions.

257 **An act to serve. Sir Veerasamy Ringadoo.**
Edited by S. Gayan.   Rose Hill, Mauritius: Editions de L'Océan Indien, 1990. 552p.

A selection of the speeches and writings of the veteran politician who headed the Ministry of Finance among others, and is currently Governor-General of Mauritius. Sir Veerasamy has been a key figure on the political scene from the pre-independence years.

258 **Le droit à l'excès.** (The right to excess.)
Alain Gordon-Gentil.   Port Louis: Caslon Printing, 1987. 152p.

A description of the political career of Sir Gaëtan Duval, political leader and lawyer, who voted against independence for Mauritius, and was in favour of association with Great Britain and the EEC. Later, he collaborated with the governments of the post-independence period to give the country a sound economic and social base. The book is richly illustrated and in French.

259 **Peace, development and self-reliance 1982-1985.**
Anerood Jugnauth.   Rose Hill, Mauritius: Editions de l'Océan Indien, 1986. 81p.

A collection of speeches by the Mauritian Prime Minister, covering the period 1982-85. The speeches are concerned with achievements and developments in culture, politics, agriculture, the economy and living standards. Jugnauth became Prime Minister in 1982. See also the recently published *Jugnauth: PM of Mauritius* by Kevin Shillington (London: Macmillan, 1991).

260 **Mauritius; the politics of change.**
A. Ramaoutar Mannick.   Mayfield College, East Sussex, England: Dodo Books, 1989. 172p.

A collection of essays by A.R. Mannick of the Department of Social Studies, Mayfield College, East Sussex, England, covering the colonial period, the political, social and economic development of Mauritius, the Diego Garcia issue, and more recent political changes in the country. This book will be of special interest to the student of contemporary Mauritian politics.

261 **Le souffle de la libération/40 ans de Travailliste (1936-1976).** (The wind of liberation – 40 years of the Labour Party [1936-1976].)
Mauritian Labour Party.   Port Louis: Mauritian Labour Party, 1976. 56p.

The book is written by the party which brought Mauritius to independence. It recounts its own birth, evolution, ideology, affiliations and role in the development of the country. It is profusely illustrated with photographs of the political leaders and pictures of Labour Party activities in Mauritius.

262 **Mauritius: cultural marginalism and political control.**
London: School of Oriental & African Studies, Centre of South Asian Studies, 1977. 12p.

This paper was presented at a seminar on language, religion, political identity and social conditions for the minorities.

263 **Our freedom. Sir Seewoosagur Ramgoolam.**
Edited by Anand Mulloo. New Delhi: Vision Books, 1982. 192p.
A collection of the speeches and writings of Mauritius's former Prime Minister and Governor-General, highlighting his political philosophy and drawing the background against which he struggled to obtain freedom for his country. The context of each speech and article is briefly explained. It is illustrated with nine photographs.

264 **L'Ile Maurice l'an 2000.** (Mauritius in the year 2000.)
Edited by Devendra Nath Varma. Port Louis: The Editor, 1985. 7p.
This short piece is 'a project for popular democracy', namely Varma's plan 'for a direct, popular, efficient and efficacious democracy'.

265 **Profiles of great Mauritians/Curé, Anquetil, Rozemont, Seeneevassen.**
Moonindra Nath Varma. Mauritius: The Author, 1981. 75p.
Biographical portraits of four Mauritians of the 1940s and 1950s who were prominent in the struggle for constitutional change, political rights and eventual independence. Dr. Maurice Curé (1886-1978) was the founder and first president of the Mauritius Labour Party (MLP), the main political party in the country's post-war and early independence history; Emmanuel Jean Baptiste Anquetil (1885-1946) was a powerful trade union leader; Guy Rozemont (1915-56) was a pioneer of the MLP, of which he was leader from 1947 to 1956; Renganaden Seeneevassen (1910-58) was a prominent figure of the MLP, and a lawyer and former Minister of Education. Black-and-white photographs are included.

266 **Rise and fall of three leaders/Bissoondoyal, Mohamed, Koenig.**
Moonindra Nath Varma. Mauritius: The Author, 1981. 73p.
An outline of the life, work and involvement in public life of three leaders who were deeply involved in the political and constitutional development of Mauritius. The politicians are: Sookdeo Bissoondoyal (1908-77), Jules Koenig (1902-68) and Abdul Razack Mohamed (1906-78). Each of them represented a particular community; Koenig was associated with the Franco–Mauritians, Mohamed with the Muslims and Bissoondoyal with the Hindu masses of rural areas. Varma explains how ethnicity and communal appurtenance were their political base; and how their rise and fall was attributed therefore to sectional interests. There are three photographs.

267 **Anerood Jugnauth – le premier ministre du changement.** (Anerood Jugnauth – Prime Minister of change.)
Le Nouveau Militant. Port Louis: Lemwee Graphics, 1982. 98p.
A biography of the Prime Minister, his childhood and adolescence at Palma, his political career, his participation in the struggle for independence and his style of leadership. It is told against a background of the political, social, economic and cultural history of the country as seen by the Mauritian Militant Movement, under whose banner Jugnauth first became Prime Minister in 1982.

268 **M.M.M. 1969-1989/20 ans d'histoire.** (MMM 1969-89/twenty years of history.)
Malenn Oodiah. Port Louis: Electronic Graphic Systems, 1989. 221p.
The book traces the origins and evolution of one of the Mauritian political parties of the post-independence era, the MMM (Mouvement Militant Mauricien). It deals with the party's ideology and personalities, and is written in a lively and essentially sympathetic style. The book contains 115 pictures.

269 **Our struggle.**
Seewoosagur Ramgoolam. New Delhi: Vision Books, 1982. 208p. bibliog.
Sir Seewoosagur Ramgoolam's own account of Mauritius's struggle for independence. The late Sir Seewoosagur was the dominant figure in Mauritian politics from the pre-independence period to the early 1980s. There is a useful index.

270 **L'appel aux urnes.** (The call to vote.)
Louis Rivaltz Quenette. Moka, Mauritius: Mahatma Gandhi Institute, 1986. 178p. bibliog.
This is an important work for the study of the evolution of human rights in Mauritius. An enlarged and revised edition of the author's *Le combat réformiste* published in 1980, the book describes the events in the second half of the 19th century concerning the struggle for a change in the constitutional *status quo* of coloured people on the island. The 'general population' wanted to participate in the administration and government of the country. Bibliographical footnotes and appendices are included, with photographs of the political leaders of the time.

271 **Electoral boundaries commission report.**
J.A. Robert. Port Louis: Government Printer, 1987. 80p.
This is a report by the Chairman of the Commission on a review of the electoral constituencies' boundaries. The study was carried out in 1986. Access to political power in Mauritius has always been through the electoral system.

272 **Ramgoolam.**
Sydney Selvon. Stanley, Rose Hill, Mauritius: Editions de l'Océan Indien, 1986. 151p.
This biography of Ramgoolam as a politician, founder of the nationalist movement and leader of the Labour Party was published as a tribute following his death in 1985. The struggle for independence is described through his life. Sir Seewoosagur Ramgoolam was the first Prime Minister of independent Mauritius.

Mauritius. Democracy and development in the Indian Ocean.
See item no. 3.

Linguistic diversity and the quest for national identity: the case of Mauritius.
See item no. 214.

Le Socialiste. (The Socialist.)
See item no. 478.

Le Rassembleur. (The Gatherer.)
See item no. 484.

Le Militant Magazine. (Militant Magazine.)
See item no. 512.

Regional

273 **Self-determination in the Western Indian Ocean.**
Philip M. Allen.   New York: Carnegie Endowment for International
Peace in International Conciliation (no. 560), 1966. 74p. map.

A short account of the rise of nationalism and self-determination in four Indian Ocean
island territories, including Mauritius. The author covers UN concerns, decolonization
and regionalism, and discusses the special circumstances of Mauritius (and the other
islands) in the regional context.

274 **The United States on Diego Garcia, a question of limits.**
Ryan J. Barilleaux.   *Air University Review*, vol. 29, no. 3 (1978).
p. 26-33. bibliog.

The author argues for the limitation of the military facilities on Diego Garcia, but
presents the counter-argument as well. A chart shows Diego Garcia's geographical
location.

275 **The problem of Mauritius sovereignty over the Chagos Archipelago and
the militarization of the Indian Ocean.**
A. Chellapermal.   Perth, Australia: University of Western Australia,
Western Australian Institute of Technology, Western Australian
College of Advanced Education and Murdoch University, 1984. 23p.
map. bibliog.

A review of American, British and Mauritian involvement in the setting up of Diego
Garcia as a US military base. The author was a representative of the Mauritius–Indian
Ocean Committee.

276 **United States policy options in the Western Indian Ocean.**
Michael F. Cordasco, Jr.   Monterey, California: Naval Postgraduate
School, 1982. 134p. bibliog.

An examination of the main Indian Ocean states from a commercial and economic
standpoint, against their regional background. This is followed by an analysis of
American interests and strategic options in the area. Written as a thesis, the paper
reaches positive conclusions about American policy in the Indian Ocean.

277 **The Indian Ocean: its political, economic and military importance.**
Edited by Alvin J. Cottrell, R.M. Burrell. London, New York:
Praeger, 1973. 2nd ed. 457p. bibliog.

A collection of papers discussed at a conference held in Washington in 1971, under the
auspices of the Center for Strategic and International Studies of Georgetown
University. The papers look at the Indian Ocean region as an integrated area of
strategic importance, particularly after the retreat of the British Royal Navy and the
subsequent pressure of the US and the USSR. Auguste Toussaint's article 'Shifting
power balances in the Indian Ocean' and T.B. Millan's paper 'Geopolitics and military/
strategic potential' are particularly relevant to Mauritius.

278 **Sea power and strategy in the Indian Ocean.**
Alvin J. Cottrell (et al.). Beverly Hills, California; London: Sage,
1981. 135p. bibliog.

A collaboration by a number of naval experts, ranging from a historical perspective on
sea power in the region, to the growth of big-power rivalries, the development of the
island of Diego Garcia as an American military base, and later political developments
in the region.

279 **Shore up the Indian Ocean.**
Steven J. Dunn. *U.S. Naval Institute Proceedings*, vol. 110/9/979
(1984), p. 131-32.

Written from an American viewpoint, this is a call for additional military facilities on
Diego Garcia in order to ensure that America would not be caught napping in the
event of a regional conflict. The book is essentially an examination of military
resources, and makes recommendations for their improvement.

280 **Diego Garcia: the Seabees at work.**
Kirby Harrison. *U.S. Naval Institute Proceedings*, vol. 105/8/918
(1979), p. 53-61.

A mainly pictorial account of the American construction of the military base on Diego
Garcia between 1971 and 1979. It includes photographs of the construction battalions
at work, and illustrations of the island itself.

281 **Diego Garcia: the militarization of an Indian Ocean island.**
Jooneed Khan. In: *African islands and enclaves.* Edited by Robin
Cohen. Beverley Hills, California; London; New Delhi: Sage, 1983,
p. 165-93. bibliog.

This book covers the history of the Chagos Archipelago (of which Diego Garcia forms
part). It explains how the British Indian Ocean Territory was created, and how Diego
Garcia was ceded to the US as a military base.

282 **Ceding territory and uprooting people to realize independence: Mauritius, Diego Garcia, and the Ilois community.**
Joel Larus.   Perth, Australia: University of Western Australia, Western Australian Institute of Technology, Western Australian College of Advanced Education and Murdoch University, 1984. 17p.
A paper dealing with the negotiations which led to the departure of the *Ilois* people from Diego Garcia for Mauritius, the establishment of an American military base there, and the creation of the British Indian Ocean Territory, and which brought about the independence of Mauritius. The paper was presented at the Second International Conference on Indian Ocean Studies held at Perth, Western Australia, 5-12 December 1984.

283 **Diego Garcia: political clouds over a vital U.S. base.**
Joel Larus.   *Strategic Review*, vol. 10, no. 1 (1982), p. 44-45.
This article explains how American interests in Diego Garcia developed and how the island became a military base. It goes on to discuss the British Labour Party's attempt to stop the move and the Mauritian government's subsequent grievances over it.

284 **Negotiating independence? Mauritius and Diego Garcia.**
Joel Larus.   *Round Table*, no. 294 (1985), p. 132-45.
An account of the findings of a Mauritian Select Committee set up in 1982, following a change of government in Mauritius to inquire into the circumstances under which the Chagos Archipelago, including Diego Garcia, was cut off from Mauritius in 1965. The US were to subsequently build a military base on Diego Garcia, leased from Britain as part of the British Indian Ocean Territory. The explanation that the then Prime Minister of Mauritius, Sir Seewoosagur Ramgoolam, made an arrangement with Britain in order to facilitate Mauritius's independence is examined.

285 **Diego Garcia: a contrast to the Falklands.**
John Madeley.   London: Minority Rights Group, 1982. 2nd ed. 16p. map. bibliog. (Report no. 54).
Co-chairman of the liberal party's group on North–South issues, John Madeley here brings attention to the plight of the Diego Garcians, who left their homeland for exile in Mauritius when it was leased to the USA for a naval base.

286 **Diego Garcia: an Indian Ocean storm center.**
John Madeley.   *Round Table*, no. 283 (1981), p. 253-57.
An examination of the negotiations between Britain, the United States and the Mauritian government leading to the creation of the British Indian Ocean Territory, the removal of the people of Diego Garcia to Mauritius and the lease of part of Diego Garcia to America for the establishment of a military base. The subsequent treatment of the *Ilois* (the Diego Garcians who were displaced) and British/American dealings are also covered.

287 **Diego Garcia and Africa's security.**
Oye Ogunbadejo. *Third World Quarterly*, vol. 4, no. 1 (1982),
p. 104-20. map.

An examination of the American presence in the Indian Ocean, focused on the Diego
Garcia military base, together with other agreements made with African governments.
Seen in the context of the Cold War, the book also discusses the influence of big-power
rivalries on inter-African disputes.

288 **The politics of the Western Indian Ocean islands.**
John M. Ostheimer, Philip M. Allen, Martin Adeney, W.K. Carr.
New York: Praeger, 1975. 227p. maps. bibliog.

A number of articles by individual authors, starting with a chapter on the sociological
and political effects of island isolation. There is a chapter on Mauritius covering
political movements, and also some information on the economy, transport and tourist
facilities.

289 **Diego Garcia.**
Paul B. Ryan. *U.S. Naval Institute Proceedings*, vol. 110/9/979 (1984),
p. 132-36.

The American acquisition of the greater part of the island of Diego Garcia as a military
base is described in detail, together with an account of those who opposed the move
and why they did so.

290 **Politics of the Indian Ocean.**
K. Rajendra Singh. Delhi: Thomson Press, 1974. 231p. maps. bibliog.

This is an examination of big-power rivalries in the Indian Ocean, seen against the
background of the development of modern weapons systems, including air, land and
sea-based missile systems, and the importance of Diego Garcia as a strategic base. The
period covered is from the end of the Second World War until the mid-1970s.

Constitution and Legal System

291 Our constitution.
Somdath Bhuckory.   Port Louis: Mauritius Printing, 1971. 115p.
bibliog.
This was originally published as a series of articles in the newspaper *Advance*, at a time when constitutional changes were thought inevitable due to the socio-economic crisis in the country, soon after independence (1968). It was aimed at sensitizing public opinion to the changes in the face of political opposition. Extensive footnotes give more information.

292 The law of Mauritius and the Seychelles.
Michael Bogdan.   Lund, Sweden: Juristiforlaget, 1989. (Skrifter utgivna av Juridiska Foreningen i Lund, no. 106).
A study of two small mixed legal systems, a legacy of the two colonial powers, British and French, that administered the islands in their early history. Much of this mixture has survived to the present day though both countries are now independent.

293 Democratic government in Mauritius.
Luckeenarainsing Bucktowar.   Port Louis, Mauritius: Rainbow Printing, 1979. 150p.
A straightforward analysis and discussion of the 1968 constitution, describing the role, functions and structure of the three main components – executive, legislative and judiciary. It explains the working of parliamentary democracy in Mauritius, and examines the philosophy behind the system. There are eight photographs.

294 **Labour laws.**
Compiled by B.H. Colin. Port Louis: Government Printer, 1915.
374p.

A compilation of the laws relative to master and servants; the immigration and poor law departments, including decisions of the supreme court; notes on game and the fishing laws; and a summary of the sanitary laws.

295 **Labour laws.**
J.G. Daly (et al.). Port Louis: Government Printer, 1880. [n.p.]

The 'Final report of the commission appointed by his honor the officer administering the government by proclamation No. 2 of 16th January 1879 and No. 10 of 27th February 1879 to frame for the approval of his Excellency the governor in executive council regulations under articles 196, 280, 281 and 282 of the labour law ordinance No. 12 of 1878'.

296 **L'Ile Maurice.** (Mauritius.)
Louis Favoreu. In: *Encyclopédie politique et constitutionelle.* Paris:
Institut International d'Administration Publique, Edition Berger-
Levrant, 1970. 119p. bibliog.

A survey of Mauritian society, including a brief account of the island's political and constitutional history to 1968 when the island achieved its independence. There is also a description and explanation of the functions of the executive, legislature and judiciary and the organisation of power, and a picture of the diversity of races, language and culture. The political parties and local government are also discussed.

297 **Real facts concerning the reform movement in Mauritius.**
A.F. Fokeer. Port Louis: Standard Printing Establishment, 1919. 73p.

An informative and readable book, useful to the historian and students of history and constitution evolution in Mauritius. It gives a vivid picture of society and events of the 1920s, and retraces the history and constitutional evolution of the Colony as it affected the different ethnic groups (Franco–Mauritians, coloured and Indo–Mauritians) from the time of Governor Napier Broome (1881). The author deplores the feeling of antagonism that had developed between the whites and the coloured. The Constitutional Reform Movement of the 1920s is fully described, and its proposals for change are discussed.

298 **Revised laws of Mauritius 1981.**
Ministry of Justice. Port Louis: Government of Mauritius, 1982.
5 vols.

This is an official publication under the Revision of Laws Act, in English. Volume 1 contains 622p.; 2, 810p.; 3, 669p.; 4, 515p.; 5, 625p. One of the amended laws in 1981 was the Forestry Department Act.

299 **Mauritius: law of criminal procedure.**
Carleton W. Kenyon. Washington, DC: Law Library, Library of
Congress, 1983. 45p.

This study was prepared for the Department of the Navy, Office of the Judge
Advocate General.

300 **La vie constitutionnelle et politique de l'Ile Maurice 1945 à 1968.**
(Constitutional and political life in Mauritius from 1945 to 1968.)
Jean-Claude Leblanc. Antananarivo, Madagascar: Annales de
l'Université de Madagascar, 1969. 176p. bibliog.

This work was originally submitted as a thesis to the Faculty of Law and Economics of
the University of Madagascar. Leblanc describes the stages of constitutional
development that culminated in the 1968 independent Mauritius constitution, and
discusses the social, cultural, economic and political implications of the changes
introduced at each stage. He also looks at the role of political parties and pressure
groups in the context of a multiracial society.

301 **Parliament in Mauritius.**
Hansraj Mathur. Rose Hill, Mauritius: Editions de l'Océan Indien,
1991. 321p. bibliog.

An outline of the origin, nature and functions, and evolution of parliament in
Mauritius from 1810 to 1990. It describes the transfer of power from the British
monarch to the people, and the establishment of parliamentary democracy on the
Westminster model in Mauritius. The electoral system, the best-loser system, the role
of the speaker and the Mauritius Legislative Assembly are fully described. It also
discusses the balance of power between the executive and the legislative, and the role
of parliament in a democracy in ensuring transparency and accountability. General
notes on election results and tables of statistics are also included. A serious book, it is
the standard work for the study of parliamentary evolution in Mauritius.

302 **Notice on procedure under a ministerial system in Mauritius (Secretariat
circular No. 8 of 1957).**
Mauritius Colonial Secretariat's Office. Port Louis: Government
Printer, 1957. 8p.

The ministerial system was set up in Mauritius in 1957. It represented an important
development in the island's constitutional history, and a definite step towards self-
government.

303 **Sessional papers/Mauritius Legislative Council (official reports).**
Mauritius Legislative Council. Port Louis: Government Printer,
1951–. (1st Issue).

A collection of irregular economic and political correspondence and reports relating to
constitutional development in Mauritius. It is useful as primary source material for
studies on the island's constitutional evolution and its implications in a multiracial
society. It is available at the Mauritius Archives and the University of Mauritius.

304 **Les constitutions de l'Ile Maurice.** (The constitutions of Mauritius.)
D. Napal.   Port Louis: Mauritius Printing, 1962. 150p. bibliog.

This book is a compilation of all the documents relating to the constitutional changes that have taken place from the beginning of the French colonial regime (1723) to 1958. A general introduction on the constitutional and legal history of the island is followed by its development in chronological order. Included are documents relating to the revolutionary regime of 1789, the dictatorship under Napoleon (1803), and the beginning of the British colonial era in 1810 ('l'acte de capitulation de 1810'). This is an important constitutional/legal study, written in French.

305 **Manilall M. Doctor/Pioneer of Indo–Mauritian emancipation.**
D. Napal.   Port Louis: Manilall Memorial Committee, 1963. 213p.

A semi-biographical work which attempts an assessment of Manilall Mangalall Doctor's contribution to the political and constitutional development of Mauritius. At the beginning of the 20th century, the Indo–Mauritian immigrants and their descendants formed about fifty per cent of the population and were the most underprivileged section of society. Manilall Doctor (1881-1956), an Indian barrister, who was sent to Mauritius in 1907 by Mahatma Gandhi, fought hard to obtain justice for the workers in the courts, and worked indefatigably to instil political consciousness among a group, many of whom had started believing that they were born to serve. Back in India in 1910, he brought their case before the Indian National Congress and pressed for the stoppage of Indian workers' recruitment for Mauritius. A number of photographs are included.

306 **The Mauritius Constitution Order, 1966.**
Police Service Commission Regulations.   Port Louis: Government Printing, 1967. 19p.

A pre-independence document which is relevant to any in-depth study of the Mauritian constitution.

307 **Le problème constitutionnel de L'Ile Maurice.** (The constitutional problem of Mauritius.)
Jean-Marie Rainaud.   Aix-en-Provence, France: Editions UJAS, Annales de la Faculté de Droit et des Sciences Economiques, 1965. 39p.

This memoir gives a clear picture of the state of affairs in the 1960s, especially during the years preceding independence (1960-67). The various political factions and parties exploited communalism on the issue of independence for Mauritius. Both the Independence Party (Labour and IFB and CAM) and the Opposition (PMSD), which struggled for Association with Great Britain, gambled with the communal feelings of the population to win their cause. The author warns the population against independence, basing his arguments upon socio-economic factors such as unemployment, overpopulation, underdevelopment, communalism and the problems associated with it.

308   **The constitution/Mauritian law: its legal aspect and political philosophy.**
Doorgesh Ramsewak.   Port Louis: The Author, 1991. 177p.
In this work the author provides a description of the constitutional machinery of the
state. He goes on to examine and analyse the relationship between the state and the
people, with respect to the people's rights and constitutional duties.

309   **Le combat réformiste.** (The Reform struggle.)
Louis Rivaltz Quenette.   Port Louis: Imprimerie Père Laval, 1980.
141p. bibliog.
This book deals with the political and constitutional development of Mauritius from
1831 to 1886. The intellectual élites of the coloured community militate for their rights,
demanding a new constitution that will give them the right to participate in the political
and financial affairs of the colony. Although the work is aimed at historians,
particularly those interested in the political and constitutional history of Mauritius,
nonetheless students and the general public too will find it very informative as it lays
the basis for further research on the period.

310   **The Mauritius laws 1990.**
Compiled by L.E. Venchard, A.H. Angelo.   Port Louis: Best
Graphics, 1990. vol. I, 717p.; vol. II, 750.; vol. III, 759p.; vol. IV,
744p.
A collection of constitutional documents and the statutes of Mauritius as at 1 January
1990. It was compiled with the approval of the Attorney-General of Mauritius, and
consolidated and edited in the Victoria Law Faculty of the University of Wellington,
New Zealand. L.E. Venchard is a former Solicitor-General of Mauritius, and A.H.
Angelo, Professor of Law at Wellington University.

311   **Subsidiary legislation of Mauritius 1988.**
Compiled by L.E. Venchard, A.H. Angelo.   Port Louis: Best
Graphics, 1988. 3 vols.
In English, this official publication comprises three volumes, with 618, 693 and 541
pages respectively. It is a compilation of all the subsidiary legislation dealt with in
Mauritius up to 1987.

312   **Problems of constitutional reform in Jamaica, Mauritius and Trinidad,
1880-95.**
H.A. Will.   London: University of London, Institute of
Commonwealth Studies, 1896. 16p. (Reprint Series no. 28).
This study is reprinted from the *English Historical Review* (vol. 81, no. 321 [October,
1896]).

L'Ile Maurice et la révolution française. (Mauritius and the French
Revolution.)
See item no. 153.

British Mauritius: 1810-1948.
See item no. 172.

The revision movement (and the present state of political affairs in Mauritius).
See item no. 250.

The Environment Protection Act 1991: Act no. 34 of 1991.
See item no. 376.

Bar Chronicle.
See item no. 500.

Administration

313 An outline of local government.
Somdath Bhuckory.   Port Louis: Association of Urban Authorities, 1970. 125p.

A series of lectures which the author delivered to officers of the five urban local authorities in 1966/67, with a completely new chapter entitled 'Means to Ends'. It is compiled in book form, with notes and comments. It outlines the history of local government in Mauritius and explains the relationship between central government and local authorities. The urban authorities – their history, structure and functions – are fully dealt with. Election of members to council, councillors' work and responsibility are also explained, along with finance and control by central government. There is also much information on the history, structure and function of local government in rural areas. This is mainly a book of special interest.

314 Commission of inquiry on allegations of fraud and corruption made against ministers and officials of the government.
Hurrylall Goburdhun.   Port Louis: Government Printer, 1985. 9p.

A report of the above-mentioned commission on corruption in politics and the government.

315 The colonial empire and its civil service.
Charles Jeffries.   London: Cambridge University Press, 1938. 259p. map.

Mauritius and its dependencies are also included in this survey. After an introduction entitled 'The colonial empire' the book is divided into two parts: development of the Civil Service and the Colonial Service today. It gives details of the general structure of the service, the conditions of employment as well as the organization and functions of the Colonial Office in London. There are several mentions of Mauritius.

316 **Administration reports laid before the Council of Government during
the session . . .**
Government of Mauritius. Port Louis: Government Printer, 1879-
1932. annual.

A collection of annual departmental reports, presented to the Council by the Colonial
Secretary's Office. It is bound in yearly instalments, and is available at the Mauritius
Archives; most issues are also at the Library of Congress in Washington.

317 **Development of rural local government in Mauritius.**
Government of Mauritius. Port Louis: Government Printer, 1956.
12p.

This is a government debates' report (Sessional paper no. 2 of 1956) of the pre-
independence period.

318 **The development of local government in Mauritius.**
Mahatma Gandhi Institute. Moka, Mauritius: Mahatma Gandhi
Institute Press, 1982. 39p.

An authoritative book on the development and function of local authorities, urban as
well as rural.

319 **Report of the public and police service commissions.**
Port Louis: Government Printer, [1990]. 40p.

A factual and statistical document covering the period 1986-89. It looks at the
establishment of the commissions, with a brief note on their purpose. A number of
tables are included, mostly on recruitment and training.

L'administration française de l'Ile Maurice et ses archives (1721-1810).
(French administration of Mauritius and its archives [1721-1810].)
See item no. 164.

Government Gazette of Mauritius.
See item no. 470.

The Economy

General

320 **Indian Ocean islands' development.**
Edited by R.T. Appleyand, R.N. Ghosh. Perth, Australia. University
of Western Australia, Centre for Research on Migration and
Development, 1988. 236p.
This monograph on economic development in the Indian Ocean islands of Mauritius,
the Comoros, the Seychelles and the Maldives examines the situation regarding
agriculture, industrialization, fisheries, tourism and macroeconomic policies. They are
all small island economies.

321 **A guide for use by committees of co-operative credit societies.**
M. Burrenchobay. Port Louis: Modern Printing, 1950. 13p.
A comprehensive guide for the administration of cooperative credit societies of the
unlimited liability type. Burrenchobay has also published *A short account of the co-
operative credit societies movement in Mauritius and the legislation by which it is
controlled*, (Port Louis: General Printing & Stationery, 1944), in which he covers all
the important points of credit societies in Mauritius and their role in the Mauritian
economy.

322 **Dix ans d'economie mauricienne (1968-1977).** (Ten years of the
economy of Mauritius [1968-77].)
Pierre Dinan. Cassis, Port Louis: Editions I.P.C. 1980. 153p. bibliog.
The decade following independence was the most difficult for the Mauritian economy.
Widespread unemployment, a monocrop economy and balance of payment deficits
created a situation that made austerity measures imperative. Diversification of the
economy and industrialization had just started and foreign investment seemed unlikely
because of the political and socio-economic instability. The author, confining himself
strictly to economic problems, makes a critical analysis, in French, of the plans and

strategies proposed to solve the problems. Sixty-four statistical tables complete the study.

323 **Madagascar, Mauritius, Seychelles, Comoros. Country Report.**
Economist Intelligence Unit. London: The Author, 1966–. quarterly.

A country report which contains an analysis of the economic and political trends in the above countries, published quarterly. The 1990 (no. 2) edition comprised sixty pages, and included an appendix of quarterly economic activity and foreign trade for each country. The general information and figures supplied are reliable.

324 **Mauritius, Seychelles, Country profile: 1990-91.**
Economist Intelligence Unit. London: The Author. 1967–. annual.

An annual survey of political and economic development. This starts with some basic data followed by details of the current political situation. Other aspects covered include Mauritian society, literacy rate, tourism, transport and communications, currency, trade and investment regulations. The 1990 edition comprised, sixty-five pages and a map of Africa with the southwest Indian Ocean islands.

325 **Successful stabilization and recovery in Mauritius.**
Ravi Gulhati, Raj Nallari. Washington, DC: Economic Development Institute of the World Bank, 1990. 90p. (Analytical Case Studies, no. 5).

This keenly researched presentation includes much statistical information. The authors examine political factors as well as the three main sectors of the Mauritian economy – sugar, manufacturing and tourism.

326 **The Indian Ocean in focus.**
International Conference on Indian Ocean Studies. Perth, Australia: Perth Building Society, 1979. [n.p.]

The inaugural conference organized by the University of Western Australia and the Western Australian Institute of Technology resulted in extensive and useful documentation on the Indian Ocean. This publication is a collection of the papers, bound in one volume. Sections cover the environment and resources; trade and development; the history of commercial exchange and maritime transport; international politics; cultural exchanges and influences; archives and resources for study; and comparative education.

327 **Finance and economy – flashback and prospects (1989-1990).**
Edited by Jeeanendra Neewoor. Port Louis: Government Publications, 1990. 65p.

This pamphlet gives an account of the development process and emphasizes the need to strengthen the island's resources so as to meet the increasingly difficult challenges ahead. The author has compiled extracts from a number of articles and speeches on the finance and economy of the island and has included excerpts from official and press reports on the role of Offshore Banking and the Stock Exchange.

328 **Mauritius Chamber of Commerce and Industry.**
Mauritius: Mauritius Chamber of Commerce and Industry, 1989.
annual. 70p.
The 1989 report provides a statistical record of the economy, including sections on employment, finance, transport, sea cargo, tourism, imports and exports, and a membership list. There are also tables on foreign trade, GNP, balance of payments, the inflation rate and other information of use to businesspersons and economists. The 1990 report had not yet been published.

329 **Industrial adjustment in sub-Saharan Africa.**
Edited by Gerald M. Meier, William F. Steel. Oxford: Oxford
University Press, 1989. 312p. bibliog.
Meier and Steel et al. have put together a valuable collection of papers by World Bank and UN staff and other experts in individual African countries. The first two chapters provide an overview and 'Strategic Orientations', and there is one specific article on 'Export-led growth in Mauritius' (World Bank staff).

330 **Mauritius: managing success.**
World Bank. Washington, DC: The Author, 1989. 162p. map.
(World Bank Country Study).
This World Bank report is a wide-ranging and detailed examination of Mauritius's economy, sources and preconditions for growth, industries, labour markets, and policies and prospects. It is valuable for anyone wishing to understand thoroughly the Mauritian economy and what has made it successful. The study contains useful text tables and a statistical annex.

Mauritius.
See item no. 16.

The economic and social structure of Mauritius. Report to the governor of Mauritius.
See item no. 17.

Créoles, Indian immigrants and the restructuring of society and economy in Mauritius, 1767-1885.
See item no. 186.

Mauritius at crossroads/The industrial challenges ahead.
See item no. 368.

Employment development and economic growth in Mauritius: a projection.
See item no. 383.

Eco-Magazine de l'Economie et des Affaires. (Eco-Economic and Business Magazine.)
See item no. 501.

Development plans and policy

331 **Mauritius, economic memorandum: recent developments and prospects.**
Michel J.C. Devaux. Washington, DC: World Bank, 1983. 222p.
map. (World Bank Country Study).

A report based on the findings of a 1981 World Bank mission to review the economic situation of Mauritius and assess progress under the structural adjustment loan. The report contains a good deal of background economic material from the mid-1960s to the 1980s, and reviews prospects for 1983-86.

332 **Successful development in Africa: case studies of projects, programs and policies.**
Introduced by Earl L. McFarland, Jr. Washington, DC: World Bank, 1989. 22p.

A macro-study of Mauritius – 'A case study of the export processing zone' by Rundheersing Bheenick and Morton Owen Schapiro – is one of seven articles in this collection; all of them are worth reading.

333 **Mauritius: a strategy for survival.**
A. Ramaoutar Mannick. London: The Author, 1982. 66p.

This is the revised version of a paper delivered by the author on the 'problems of economic survival in small developing countries with special reference to Mauritius'.

334 **A call for action.**
Ministry of Economic Planning and Development. Port Louis: The Ministry, 1976. 22p.

This is a booklet that highlights the areas and need for urgent action in the 1975-80 plan for social and economic development. The first post-independence years were rife with problems of unemployment, over-population, mass emigration, and a serious economic crisis. Revenue was low and expenditure on imports high; immediate solutions were needed, hence the 'call for action'. Among the strategies were the creation of jobs, youth-training, diversification of agriculture, industrialization, tourism development and less imports.

335 **Development strategy 1971-1980.**
Ministry of Economic Planning and Development. Port Louis: The Ministry, 1970. 69p.

A description of the ten-year strategy plan for development devised by the newly independent country against a background of high unemployment. The main objectives of the plan were the creation of 130,000 new jobs with the structural changes required in the economy to generate employment opportunities; the cultivation of some 250 acres to boost crop production and the expansion of the manufacturing sector.

336 **Four year plan for social and economic development 1971-1975.**
Ministry of Economic Planning and Development.   Port Louis: The
Author, 1971. 2 vols. maps.
The first volume of this initial five-year plan of the independent government contains a
general analysis of the situation and the policies to be followed (262p.). Volume 2
gives details of the programmes and projects for the first phase of the development
strategy 1971-80.

337 **Mauritius economic survey.**
Ministry of Economic Planning and Development.   Port Louis: The
Author, 1974. 86p.
This and the survey of 1970-72 are comprehensive, and also contain information in the
form of tables and figures. More than half-way into the 1971-75 plan (which aimed at
reducing unemployment), the economy, in 1974, was vulnerable with its reliance on a
monocrop industry, dominated by sugar production, widespread unemployment and
balance of payment deficits.

338 **Mauritius: 1975-1980. Five year plan for social and economic
development.**
Ministry of Economic Planning and Development.   Port Louis: The
Author, 1976. 200p. maps.
This is the second of the five-year plans in the context of the development strategy set
out in 1970 against a background of changes in the situation after the first five years.
There are a number of tables and figures.

339 **National development plan 1988-1990.**
Ministry of Economic Planning and Development.   Port Louis: The
Author, 1988. 2 vols. maps.
The first of these shorter development plans was prepared in 1980. The highlights of
the plans in the decade were manpower development, the increasing of self-reliance,
public sector investment, industrialization and the restructuring of the sugar sector.

340 **Report of the consultation meeting on management of tuna resources of
the Indian and Pacific Oceans, Manila, Philippines, 26-29 June 1979.**
Manila: Food and Agricultural Organization of the United Nations, and
the South China Sea Fisheries Development and Coordinating
Programme, 1979. 137p.
Mauritius was represented at the 6th Joint Meeting of the Committee on Management
of Indo–Pacific Tuna at Perth, Western Australia, in 1980. This report was submitted
to that meeting, and covers a wide range of subjects including management reform in
the tuna-fishing industry and the discussion of an extended zone of jurisdiction.

Budgeting. International Monetary Fund and The World Bank.
See item no. 348.

Urban planning

341 **La Tour Koenig development study, Mauritius: final report.**
Australian Development Assistance Bureau, jointly with the
Government of Mauritius.   Adelaide, Australia: P.C. Pak-Poy &
Associates, 1981. 96p.

A study was carried out in 1979-80 for the Australian Development Assistance Bureau
and the Government of Mauritius in order to evaluate the economic and financial
feasibility of establishing low-cost residential development on a site (La Tour Koenig)
west of the capital, Port Louis. This is the consultants' report, and is of interest to
development planners. Tables and illustrations complete the study.

342 **Mauritius shelter sector analysis appendix volume.**
Office of Housing, Agency for International Development.
Washington, DC: Agency for International Development, 1978. 88p.
map. bibliog.

This volume brings together the detailed statistical information used in the 'shelter
sector' analysis carried out for the Government of Mauritius. It is valuable for its
information about the economic background of Mauritius, and local building costs and
supplies. There is also some social material, as well as tables and illustrations.

343 **A master plan for Port Louis.**
L.W. Thornton White.   Cape Town: Price Lewis & Sturrock, 1952.
90p. maps.

This report gives a fascinating history and analysis of the planning needs and problems
of the Mauritian capital which, although highly picturesque, had a policy at the time of
'anyone can build anything, anywhere, anyhow'. It makes proposals for rational
development along modern town-planning principles. Not all Professor Thornton
White's solutions were carried out. The most acceptable recommendation was the
construction of a two-lane motorway linking Port Louis via Moka with the upper part
of the Plaines Wilhems district. The construction began in 1960 and has since been
completed, greatly easing travel between the capital and the centre of the island.

The Environment Protection Act 1991: Act no. 34 of 1991.
See item no. 376.

Living in Mauritius: traditional architecture of Mauritius.
See item no. 409.

Maisons traditionnelles de l'Ile Maurice. (Traditional Mauritian houses.)
See item no. 412.

Finance

344 **Capital budget 1973-74 with memorandum (as passed by the Legislative Assembly on the 29th June, 1973).**
Port Louis: Ministry of Finance, 1973. 46p. (Mauritian Government Publications).

A yearly financial report, with appendices and a memorandum on the capital fund and revenue. The 1973 official publication includes details of various ministries' project plans being implemented or completed, in the form of tables and expenditure. The Mauritian financial year runs from July to June.

345 **A history of currency in the British colonies.**
Robert Chalmers.   Essex, England: John Drury, 1972. 496p.

The reprint of this invaluable book for the study of fiscal history includes a number of references to Mauritian currency. Chapter VI (p. 360-70) deals particularly with Mauritius. The author suggests that a lesson is to be drawn from this study in 'the futility of arbitrary endeavours to substitute an alien scheme of currency for that prescribed by trade relations'. This explains the establishment of the rupee (which is still legal tender in the country) by law as the island's standard of value in 1876, after more than fifty years of unsuccessful attempts to introduce sterling as the local currency. The book is also useful for its economic information substantiated by tables. There is an index.

346 **The control of public expenditure, Mauritius Legislative Council.**
Port Louis: Government Printer, 1957. 70p. (Sessional Paper, no. 7 [1957]).

This paper resulted from the review of the methods by which the system of financial control was to be achieved and adapted to the level of constitutional development. It outlines the procedure whereby the Legislative Council should consider and resolve all matters concerning public expenditure. It is a handbook intended as a comprehensive and authoritative document dealing with all aspects of public expenditure control in Mauritius in the financial years 1957-59.

347 **150 années de jeunesse – a history of the Mauritius Commercial Bank.**
Marcelle Lagesse. Port Louis: Mauritius Commercial Bank, 1988.
335p.

A detailed account of the foundation and evolution of the Mauritius Commercial Bank, which was founded in 1838, and its role in the economic development of Mauritius. Although published by the bank itself, and therefore uncritical, it is a useful work of reference. There are a number of illustrations and an index.

348 **Budgeting. International Monetary Fund and The World Bank.**
V. Mulloo. Port Louis: Ministry of Finance, 1988. 47p.

Mulloo, principal assistant secretary at the Ministry of Finance, examines the various aspects of budgeting – definition, role, functions, operations, structure, formulation, implementation and evaluation. He also discusses the distinct roles and functions of the IMF and the World Bank, two institutions with whom Mauritius has had a very close relationship.

349 **Financial report for the year 1987-88.**
Ministry of Finance. Port Louis: The Ministry, Sept. 1989. 160p.

A factual and analytical report at the end of the financial year (June), consisting mainly of tables, expenditure and revenue statements, assets, foreign aid and debt details. It is an annual report with the first going back to 1932.

Commerce and industry in Mauritius.
See item no. 369.

Report of the director of audit/for the year ended 30 June 1989.
See item no. 474.

Agriculture

General

350 **Bulletins of the Department of Agriculture.**
Department of Agriculture. Moka, Mauritius: Government Printer,
1914-49. (General Series; 1915-48; Scientific Series; 1915-34; Statistical
Series; 1917; Leaflet series.)
In English and French, these bulletins are available from the Mauritius Archives and
public libraries of the Department of Agriculture. They also survey forestry and
fishing.

351 **World atlas of agriculture.**
Committee for the World Atlas of Agriculture. Italy: Istituto
Geografico De Agostini with the International Association of
Agricultural Economics, 1969-76. 4 vols. maps. bibliog. (*Africa*.
vol. iv., 1976).
Mauritius is included in the *Africa* volume of this publication, together with the other
south-western Indian Ocean territories. A number of maps cover subjects such as soils,
climate and rainfall and there is a survey of land ownership, land utilization for crops,
and animal husbandry and the physical environment as well as human settlements in
each of the islands.

352 **Report on the fishery resources of Mauritius.**
James Hornell. Port Louis, Mauritius: J. Eliel Félix, Government
Printer, 1955. 35p.
The author was commissioned by the Secretary of State for the Colonies to carry out a
survey of the marine resources of Mauritius and make recommendations for their
improvement and development. The book describes the physical characteristics of the
coast and adjacent seas and the organization of the fishing industry. Among the

recommendations are the creation of a fisheries department and the establishment of a fisheries experimental station.

353 **Annual report of the agricultural services of the Ministry of Agriculture, Fisheries and Natural Resources for the year.**
Ministry of Agriculture.   Réduit, Mauritius: The Author, 1969–.

A comprehensive annual review of Mauritius's agricultural services, with many tables and statistics. The 1986 edition comprised 148 pages. The agricultural sector had a good year in 1985: sugar production rose to 646,000 tons after several successive poor harvests, which resulted from a combination of cyclones and droughts. Tea production also reached an all-time record of 8,115 tons in 1985.

354 **Seminar on agriculture diversification (August 1980) – plan of action.**
Ministry of Agriculture, Natural Resources and the Environment.
Port Louis: Government Printer, 1980.

The publication of the papers presented at this seminar, and the discussions that took place, is an attempt at sensibilization to the need to increase food production. A greater degree of self-sufficiency for Mauritius would subsequently reduce the need for food imports.

355 **La Revue Agricole de l'Ile Maurice or La Revue Agricole et Sucrière de l'Ile Maurice.** (Mauritius Agricultural Review or Mauritius Agriculture and Sugar Industry Review.)
Edited by G.A. North Coombes.   Port Louis: General Printing & Stationery, 1922-. bimonthly.

This journal appears every two months regularly. Articles are in English and French and mainly cover the subjects of soils, climate and agriculture, e.g.'La dernière coulée de laves à l'Île Maurice' ('Last lava flow in Mauritius') (1983) by R. Antoine; 'The effects of tropical cyclones on the sugar crop in Mauritius' (1957) by A.D. Swan. Articles are sometimes issued separately.

356 **Some medicinal plants of economic importance in Mauritius.**
W.T.H. Wong Ting Fook.   BSc dissertation, University of Mauritius, 1979. 160p.

A fascinating paper, in which the reader will find him/herself asking if the exploitation of medicinal plants will become an economic reality and an enterprise worth the efforts being put into it.

Climate in Mauritius.
See item no. 48.

A history of woods and forests in Mauritius.
See item no. 115.

Mauritius and the spice trade: the odyssey of Pierre Poivre.
See item no. 159.

The triumph of Jean Nicolas Céré and his Isle Bourbon collaborators.
See item no. 160.

Report of the consultation meeting on management of tuna resources of the Indian and Pacific Oceans, Philippines, 26-29 June 1979.
See item no. 340.

Report on the fishery resources of Mauritius.
See item no. 352.

Multi-criteria planning for agricultural development: a full employment strategy for Mauritius.
See item no. 384.

Land tenure/policy

357 **White paper on Crown forest land (land utilization) and forestry.**
   W. Allan, L.F. Edgerley. Port Louis: J. Eliel Félix, Government
   Printer, 1950. 37p. map.
The white paper describes and categorizes the Crown Lands which cover a little less than eighteen per cent of the total area of the island. It examines past policies, and argues that a distinct forest policy is required for the utilization and protection of the Crown forest areas. Appendices include tables giving the dates of acquisition and purchase price of Crown lands, from 1880 to 1950; a list of Crown lands to be excluded from the proposed forestry programme and reserved for tea plantations; and the classification of Crown forestlands.

358 **Précis terrier de l'Ile Maurice ou Table générale de toutes les concessions faites dans les divers districts de la colonie.** (Land distribution in
   Mauritius or General table of the concessions in all the different
   districts of the colony.)
   Adolphe Macquet. Port Louis: Cernéen, 1887. 67p.
Written in French by a prior notary, the original copy no longer exists. This is a photocopy which is to be found at the Mauritius Archives. It is an important document for any study on land policy and administration, and most useful to notaries. It is an index of all the land parcels distributed in the various districts, their size, the names of the concessionaries, and the register where all these details have been entered. There are also details about the rules pertaining to these concessions.

359 **Histoire des domaines sucriers de l'Ile Maurice.** (A history of the sugar
   estates of Mauritius.)
   Guy Rouillard. [n.p.], 1979. 516p. maps.
A handsomely presented book, lavishly illustrated in black-and-white, covering the history of the sugar estates in detail. Useful sociological information is provided about places and inhabitants.

360 **Retriangulation of Mauritius, 1934.**
V.E.H. Sanceau   Cardiff: William Lewis (Printers), 1935. 33p.

Apart from the early surveys of the island, such as the one carried out by the Abbé de La Caille (1780s) and the two complete surveys, the first one by Conal (1870-80) and the second by the Colonial Survey Section (1903-04), no other surveys had been made until this one. The surveys previously did not corroborate, and the need for a new survey was urgent as the Cadastral Section of the Public Works and Survey Department was experiencing much difficulty. All details of working, data computation, coordinates and bearings are shown in tables and diagrams. It is a highly technical report.

Sugar

361 **Lured away – the life history of Indian cane workers.**
Huguette Ly-Thio-Fane Pineo.   Moka, Mauritius: Mahatma Gandhi Institute Press, 1984. 261p.

The books tells the life history of the Indian cane workers in Mauritius with objectivity and sensitivity. The sugar industry would not have survived and developed without them. There is a long list of the historical studies carried out on the subject and documents at the end.

362 **Mauritius Sugar Industry Research Institute.**
Moka, Mauritius: MSIRI, 1958–. occasional.

Irregular articles in English and French, including 'Notes on the 1:100,000 soil map of Mauritius' by D.H. Parish and the late S.M. Feillafe (1965); 'Notes on the agro-climate map of Mauritius' by P. Halais and E.G. Davy (1969); and 'Carte pédologique de l'Ile Maurice 1:50,000' ('Pedological map of Mauritius') by P. Willaime (1984).

363 **L'Ile Maurice depuis sa conquête par l'Angleterre.** (Mauritius since its conquest by the British.)
Thomy Merven.   Port Louis: R. Ollivry, 1895. 34p.

This book is an account of the conquest of Mauritius in 1810, the development of the sugar industry and sugar production from 1818 to 1895, taxation on production accessories, and the Indian and Mauritian population.

364 **Sugar in Mauritius.**
Public Relations Office of the Sugar Industry.   Les Pailles, Mauritius: Henri & Co., 1987. 4th rev. ed. 151p. maps.

This is a comprehensive manual on the Mauritian sugar industry. It starts with a general chapter on geography, history, population, topography, climate, land use, geology and soils and climatic conditions affecting sugar production. The information provided covers the organization and structure of the industry including ownership policy, production and research, marketing and export, employment and welfare, supplies, equipment and transport, agricultural diversification on cane lands, sugar and the economy of the island. There are some useful tables and good references.

Histoire des domaines sucriers de l'Ile Maurice. (A history of the sugar estates of Mauritius.)
See item no. 359.

The Mauritius government railways and the transport of sugar by road.
See item no. 379.

Industry

General

365 Mauritius: towards an industrial training strategy.
R. Bheenick, E. Hanoomanjee.   Stanley, Rose Hill, Mauritius:
Editions de l'Océan Indien, 1988. 232p.

This is a critical review of Mauritius as a new industrialized nation. It argues that the
human resources are inadequate and the structure and organization of the industrial
activities are limited. It calls for the elaboration of an industrial training strategy to
meet the demands created by industrialization.

366 The census of industrial production, 1967-68.
Central Statistical Office.   Port Louis: Ministry of Economic Planning
and Development, 1970. annual.

A regular survey and compilation of industrial statistics for the Ministry of Economic
Planning and Development, showing the trends over the year.

367 Cargo handling and cargo loss prevention. Port Louis Harbour.
A. Naga.   Port Louis: Bahadour Printing, Pailles, 1983. 83p.

A survey and evaluation of the various devices introduced by the Mauritian Marine
Authority to prevent cargo loss, since the Authority's establishment in 1976. The book
describes the wide range of modern port facilities including deep water sheds, modern
transit sheds, and cargo handling equipment. The author discusses the plan to make
Port Louis a free port.

368 **Mauritius at the crossroads/The industrial challenges ahead.**
Ministry of Industry and Industrial Technology.   Port Louis: The
Ministry, 1990. 162p. map. bibliog.

A publication by the Ministry aimed at 'setting the platform for healthy debate on issues that touch practically every Mauritian quite closely'. The book includes a review of economic performance and a look back at industrial progress over the years. It also examines the export processing zone scheme and analyses objectives and policies. Tables and figures complete the review. Anyone interested in trade and investment in Mauritius should also consult *Mauritius Export Directory*, which is published annually by the Mauritius Export Development and Investment Authority (MEDIA).

369 **Commerce and industry in Mauritius.**
Ministry of Industry, Commerce and External Communications.   Port
Louis: The Ministry, 1967. 114p. maps.

A handbook for investors, trade organizations and businesspersons. It was produced by the Ministry in an attempt to attract investment, local as well as international, in the country as a newly independent nation. It contains commercial information and legislation as well as a chapter on 'Incentives to investment' which gives details of the facilities available to prospective entrepreneurs.

370 **Maurice guide 1971.** (Mauritius guide 1971.)
Edited by Camille Alex Moutou.   Port Louis: Standard Printing
Establishment, 1971. 497p.

This is an illustrated French-English directory of Mauritius, with details of interest to the commercial, industrial and holiday visitor. It also contains useful information about Madagascar and Réunion.

Report of the consultation meeting on management of tuna resources of the Indian and Pacific Oceans, Philippines, 26-29 June 1979.
See item no. 340.

Report on the fishery resources of Mauritius.
See item no. 352.

Mauritius Sugar Industry Research Institute.
See item no. 362.

L'Ile Maurice depuis sa conquête par l'Angleterre. (Mauritius since its conquest by the British.)
See item no. 363.

Sugar in Mauritius.
See item no. 364.

Export processing zone

371 **Wishing a future for the EPZ.**
Philippe A. Forget. Port Louis: Government Publications, 1983.
115p. bibliog.

A comprehensive array of facts and figures as a basis for suggestions with a view to revitalizing the export industry. The author demonstrates the necessity of EPZ (Export Processing Zone) activities to solve balance of payment problems and unemployment. The case for the free zone as a package of needed incentives for real and durable industrial investment is argued.

372 **Export processing zones and development: the experience of Mauritius.**
Matthew William Roberts. Bloomington, Indiana: School of Public and Environmental Affairs, Indiana University, 1988. 34p.

This is a study of the growth of industrialization, the economy and the development of Mauritius. Particular reference is made to the export processing zone, its structure, rapid expansion and current success.

Mauritius at the crossroads/The industrial challenges ahead.
See item no. 368.

Le Républicain. (The Republican.)
see item no. 493.

Zone Franche Magazine. (Free Zone Magazine.)
See item no. 502.

Tourism

373 **Islander.**
Air Mauritius Publicity Department. Port Louis: Air Mauritius, [1972-]. quarterly.

Glossy, richly illustrated and published quarterly, this is the inflight magazine of Air Mauritius, the national airline. It includes articles on the culture and history of Mauritius and other countries, aimed mainly at the tourist, with advertisements.

374 **South African tourism to the Indian Ocean islands: market survey, 1984.**
Bureau of Financial Analysis, University of Pretoria. Pretoria: The Bureau, 1984. 89p.

A survey commissioned by the University of Pretoria was sent to travel agents in South Africa to determine the need for improved air travel facilities to a number of Indian Ocean tourist resorts, including Mauritius. The conclusion was that an increase in air flights was required, and that a greater frequency of air flights was also needed for travel between South Africa and the Seychelles.

375 **International travel and tourism.**
Central Statistical Office. Rose Hill, Mauritius: Mauritius Central
Statistical Office, Ministry of Economic Planning and Development,
1974–. 43p.

A statistical study of the tourist industry primarily at a time when its importance in the
Mauritian economy was growing. It is now an annual publication.

376 **The Environment Protection Act 1991: Act no. 34 of 1991.**
Government Gazette of Mauritius: Legal Supplement, no. 72 (20 July
1991), p. 151-202.

The chapter and verse of the legal side of the Environmental Protection Act. This is
extremely important for a country whose industrial success and consequent growth in
building homes, hotels for tourism and factories, and in improving its infrastructure,
threatens to harm the environment and natural beauty of Mauritius.

377 **Airport development and future economic growth in Mauritius.**
Ministry of Economic Planning and Development. Port Louis: The
Ministry, 1982. 48p.

The plan for the development of the airport is crucial for the tourist industry and
economic growth and important with respect to diversifying the Mauritian economy.
Information is provided on the transport network and overseas communication
facilities.

Transport and Communications

378 **A history of the Mauritius government reailways (1864-1964).**
Arthur Jessop. Port Louis: The Government, 1964. 29p.
Jessop, who was transport advisor to the Mauritian government from 1953 to 1955, traces the history of the railway system on the island to its introduction in 1864. This contributed tremendously to the country's economic development, but when more convenient and cheaper means of transport came, the system was closed. This was done in stages starting from 1961, with the final line closing in 1964.

379 **The Mauritius government railways and the transport of sugar by road.**
Port Louis: Government Printer, 1962. (Sessional paper, no. 1 [1962].)
Until the 1960s, the sugar cane used to be transported to the factories by rail. With the closure of the rail system, development of the road network is envisaged.

380 **Development of roads and road traffic in Mauritius.**
Ministry of Works. Port Louis: The Author, 1973. 22p. map.
A government publication containing statistical information about Mauritius's road and traffic development, with a brief introduction. Graphs and tables are included.

381 **The 'Post Office Mauritius' and its legend.**
Alfred S. de Pitray. Rose Hill, Mauritius: Editions de l'Océan Indien, 1990. 42p.
The legend has it that the engraver of this famous stamp made an error, putting 'Post Office' instead of 'Post Paid'. No one knows if this is true, but this book examines the evidence. Another source is *Postage stamps and the empire's story* by A.O. Crane (London: Stanley Gibbons, [n.d.]. 58p.).

Edlico road atlas of Mauritius.
See item no. 75.

Mauritius guide with street maps.
See item no. 83.

South African tourism to the Indian Ocean islands: market survey, 1984.
See item no. 374.

Airport development and future economic growth in Mauritius.
See item no. 377.

Manpower and Employment

382 **Groupes progrès et liberté/'Combattre le chômage'.** (Fighting unemployment.)
Port Louis: Imprimerie Père Laval, 1981. 46p.
This pamphlet, written in French, discusses the problems of employment in Mauritius. It provides factual and statistical information about industry and employment conditions, with a conclusion presenting solutions for the future.

383 **Employment development and economic growth in Mauritius: a projection.**
Horst Seidler. Berlin: Deutsches Institut für Wirtschaftsforschung (German Institute for Economic Research), 1965. 44p. (Sessional Paper, no. 2 [1966] for the Mauritius Legislative Assembly).
This paper, written in English, was published during a period of economic difficulty when the population was increasing rapidly. It is of interest for its assessment of Mauritian needs for the future and its comments on the possibilities of industrialization, especially in partnership with international firms.

384 **Multi-criteria planning for agricultural development: a full employment strategy for Mauritius.**
J.L. Clovis Vellin, Timothy D. Mount, Thomas T. Poleman. Ithaca, New York: Department of Agricultural Economics, New York State College of Agriculture and Life Sciences, Cornell University, 1972. 90p. bibliog.
Written at a time of high unemployment in Mauritius, this is a study, adapted from Dr. Vellin's PhD thesis, of the lessons to be learnt from Mauritius's dependence on sugar-cane production. It is of interest as a snapshot of Mauritius's agricultural situation before the economy diversified.

Indian labour immigration.
See item no. 196.

The indenture system in Mauritius, 1837-1915.
See item no. 204.

Mauritius: towards an industrial training strategy.
See item no. 365.

Women in Mauritius (in figures).
See item no. 473.

Directory of training resources.
See item no. 527.

Labour Movement and Industrial Relations

385 **Le mouvement syndical à l'Ile Maurice.** (Trade unionism in Mauritius.)
Rajpalsingh Allgoo. Port Louis: Artisans & General Workers' Union, 1985. 110p.

Written in three parts, the first being about the genesis of the working class, the second about the birth of the movement with Anquetil and Rozemont and the third dealing with the trade union movements of Mauritius since the 1930s. It also discusses the role of trade unionism in post-independent Mauritius and working-class militancy. The book is written in French.

386 **From cane-field to parliament – a profile of Harryparsad Ramnarain.**
Abhimanya Annuth. New Delhi: Natraj Prakashan, 1989. 175p.

A biography of the outstanding trade unionist of the 1940s who worked to educate the workers in their rights, both labour and constitutional. His work laid the foundation for a strong Labour Party with a broad political base. The book is illustrated, and is also available in Hindi.

387 **Trade unionism in Mauritius.**
Kenneth Baker. Port Louis: J.E. Félix, Acting Government Printer, 1946. 40p.

The development of trade unionism in Mauritius closely followed the progress of politics. Labour leaders played a crucial role in the Labour Party's efforts to bring about greater emancipation, better labour laws and the workers' participation in enterprise management. This is the background against which Kenneth Baker (a union adviser sent from England in early 1945, who was instrumental in organizing the industrial associations into trade unions) sets his discussion.

388 **50 ans de lutte syndicale, 1938-1988.** (Fifty years of trade union
struggle, 1938-88.)
Chandersensing Bhagirutty.   Port Louis: Plantation Workers' Union,
1989. 108p.

A valuable history of trade unionism in Mauritius since its beginnings. The author
assesses the progress made to better the lot of the worker. This book is useful for the
general reader as well as the historian. Another useful source on trade union history is
Malen D. Oodiah's *Histoire du syndicalisme Mauricien*, (Port Louis: Royal Printing),
in which the author traces fifty years of the trade union movement in Mauritius. He
begins with the story of the slaves in the island and explains how trade unionism had a
long and difficult birth, but eventually resulted in the establishment of the Mauritian
Labour Party. Written in French, and from a Marxist standpoint, the book is
nevertheless a useful analysis for students of the trade union movement in Mauritius.

389 **Labour relations in Mauritius.**
A.K. Gujadhur, D.A. Luchmun, R. Pyneeandee.   Port Louis: The
Authors, 1983. 103p.

A background paper on labour relations in Mauritius in the context of a National
Programme on Workers' Participation as a strategy for development. It relates the
history of industrial relations in Mauritius with particular reference to collective
bargaining and workers' participation in major sectors of the Mauritian economy.

Listwar lagrev ut 1979. (An account of the August 1979 strike.)
See item no. 177.

Labour laws.
See item no. 294.

Labour laws.
See item no. 295.

Education

390 **Annual report on education for 1971.**
Ministry of Education.   Port Louis: Government Printer, 1973. 30p.
(Mauritian Government Publication).
After a brief introduction and explanation of Mauritius's education policies, the report
gives a statistical analysis of education in Mauritius. There are tables covering subjects
such as enrolment, examinations, overseas aid and teacher training.

391 **Education and the sports world.**
D. Awootar.   Mauritius: Mauritius Institute of Education, 1980. 72p.
bibliog.
A study of the problems which have hindered the effective teaching of physical
education at the primary-school level in Mauritius. The author stresses that sport
should form an integral part of education and urges the participation of women as well.

392 **Education without opportunity: education, economics and communalism
in Mauritius.**
Burton Benedict.   London: Institute of Commonwealth Studies,
University of London, 1958. p. 325-29. bibliog. (Reprint Series, no. 4).
Benedict emphasizes the political and social aspects of education in Mauritius. He
explains how the economic betterment of the Indian community was linked with their
desire to get away from the sugar industry, whose higher posts were closed to them,
and take advantage of the opportunities offered through education. Tables cover the
languages spoken by the different communities. This paper was originally published in
Human Relations, vol. xi, no. 4 (Nov. 1958).

393 **The organization of secondary and superior instruction, with especial reference to the colonies.**
Charles Bruce. London: Stanford, 1870. [n.p.].
This study contains an account of an educational experiment in the colony of Mauritius together with the programme of studies followed. Sir Charles Bruce was Governor of the island from 1897 to 1904.

394 **Rémi et Marie: petits écoliers mauriciens.** (Rémi and Marie, young Mauritian schoolchildren.)
N. Cangy, R. Des Forges, R. Lamusse, P.H. Madelaine. Paris: Fernand Nathan, 1975, 2nd ed. 64p.
A French textbook for 2nd-year primary-school children. The context of the simple French narrative is Mauritian, and Rémi and Marie use language with which Mauritian children can identify. The text is accompanied by line drawings in two colours designed to enhance the children's understanding of the text.

395 **Centre for Indian Ocean Regional Studies.**
Indian Ocean Newsletter, vol. 7, no. 1 (1987), p. 1-2.
The Centre for Indian Ocean Regional Studies (CIORS) was set up in Western Australia in 1987, and produces the academic journal *Indian Ocean Newsletter* (q.v.). This issue explains the organization and purpose of the CIORS.

396 **Issue-based Indian Ocean Network (IBION) inaugural workshop in Mauritius (1985).**
P. Chellapermal. *Indian Ocean Newsletter*, vol. 6, no. 2 (1985), p. 9, 14.
This issue of the *Indian Ocean Newsletter* (q.v.) is an account of the first Issue-based Indian Ocean Network (IBION) workshop held in Mauritius in 1985. The first themes for study were the geopolitics of the Indian Ocean, regional cooperation and economic development, regional resources and the impact of development on the environment. IBION, which is based in Mauritius, has continued its work since then, and publishes a newsletter, *Issue-based Indian Ocean Network (IBION)* (q.v.), three times a year.

397 **Participation and performance in primary schooling.**
Vinayagum Chinapah. Stockholm: University of Stockholm, Institute of International Education, 1983. 215p. (Studies in Comparative and International Education, no. 8).
This dissertation for the doctor's degree in social science at the Institute of International Education, University of Stockholm, is a study of educational equality of opportunity in Mauritius.

398 **Educational development: the small states of the Commonwealth.**
Education Programme Human Resource Development Group,
Commonwealth Secretariat. London: Commonwealth Secretariat
Publications, 1986. [n.p.].

This is the report of a pan-Commonwealth experts' meeting in Mauritius to discuss
national and educational development in small states. The meeting was held in
November 1985. It examined the particular educational needs of small states and
considered ways to help them. The eight chapters cover the following: economic, social
and political contexts for educational development; the school system – the impact of
smallness of scale; post-secondary education in small states; education in archipelago
countries, distance education for small states; dependence, independence and
interdependence; external assistance for education, and proposals for action.

399 **Mauritius: the research environment.**
P. Heeralall, I. Dassyne. Port Louis: Centre de Documentation de
Recherches et de Formation Indienocéaniques (CEDREFI), 1990. 62p.

This is based on a study (1985) of the structure and state of research activities in
Mauritius. The aim was to improve the effectiveness of the International Development
Research Centre's strategy and assistance for consolidating endogenous research
capabilities in developing countries with populations of less than ten million.

400 **Indian Ocean islands naturally: a review of developments.**
Madeleine Ly-Tio-Fane. *Indian Ocean Newsletter*, vol. 5, no. 2 (Dec.
1984), p. 1-4.

The author had an interest in long-term conservation plans and educational
programmes to protect the natural surroundings, and her bibliography was partly
written in support of them. It covers the history of early researches and later scientific
studies.

401 **Committee of enquiry into the non-government and non-aided secondary
schools of Mauritius.**
Ministry of Education and Cultural Affairs. Port Louis: The Ministry,
[n.d.]. 33p.

The Committee's Chairman, Frank Richard, was the Chief Education Officer of
Mauritius. The report studies the growth of private schools in Mauritius, their
standards and the qualification of their teachers, and gives rules for opening hours and
admissions, and makes recommendations for improvements. Appendices cover the
growth of private schools, the numbers of teachers and analyses of examination results.

402 **Biennial report on education.**
Ministry of Education, Arts and Culture. Port Louis: The Ministry,
1988. 72p.

A survey and record of educational aims and priorities, legislation, scholarships and
staffing, covering the period 1987-88. It also includes a table giving details of the
expenditure on education with the sources of revenue. There are numerous other
tables and statistical information. The outer islands are also included.

403 **The development of education in Mauritius 1710-1976.**
Ramesh Ramdoyal. Moka, Mauritius: Mauritius Institute of
Education, 1977. 180p. map.
The book covers Mauritian education in (a) the 18th and first half of the 19th centuries; (b) the second half of the 19th century; and (c) from 1900. A carefully researched and important study, it is also of interest to present-day educational planners. There is an index and tables.

404 **The Second International Conference on Indian Ocean studies, Perth, Western Australia, December 1984.**
Peter Reeves. *Indian Ocean Newsletter*, vol. 6, no. 1 (June 1985), p. 1, 8-9, 11.
The conference planned a Centre for Indian Ocean Studies, and this issue of the *Indian Ocean Newsletter* (q.v.) is a review of the conference's proceedings. It includes a list of delegates and a review of the papers submitted.

405 **L'oeuvre du Révérend Jean Lebrun à l'Île Maurice.** (The work of Reverend Jean Lebrun in Mauritius.)
Louis Rivaltz Quenette. Port Louis: Regent Press, [n.d.]. 244p.
This is the life history of Lebrun (1789-1865), a French priest, who pressed for further action by the British administration to provide education for Mauritian children. Upon his arrival in Mauritius, he started mission schools where poor children received some elementary education. Lebrun also worked for the abolition of slavery. The story is told with sensitivity, and is illustrated.

406 **Education.**
Edited by B. Seebaluck. Mauritius: Editions de l'Océan Indien, 1985-. monthly.
Written in English and French. Concerned with educational issues and achievements, the magazine features articles on such topics as music and education, language teaching and computers.

407 **CEDREFI – Centre de Documentation, de Recherches, et de Formation Indienocéaniques.** (Centre for Documentation, Research, and Training on the South West Indian Ocean.)
Pierce Yin. Port Louis: CEDREFI, 1981. 4p.
CEDREFI, which was formed in 1981 in Mauritius, documents studies in the islands of the south-west Indian Ocean, and carries out research and training programmes. This pamphlet explains its work.

Nouvelle géographie à l'usage des écoles de l'Ile Maurice. (New geography for Mauritian students.)
See item no. 28.

Language teaching in the Indian Ocean.
See item no. 216.

The Arts

Visual arts

408 **Panorama de la peinture mauricienne.** (Panorama of Mauritian painting.)
Georges André Decotter. Rose Hill, Mauritius: Editions de l'Océan Indien, 1986 and 1989. 2 vols.

An important work, handsomely illustrated in colour, covering Mauritian painting from 1800-1975 and from 1975-86. The author sets out to inspire the young present-day artists of Mauritius by discussing the artistic heritage of the past.

409 **Living in Mauritius: traditional architecture of Mauritius.**
Isabelle Desvaux de Marigny, Jean-François Koenig, Christian Saglio, Henriette Valentin Lagesse, translated from the French by Isabelle Desvaux de Marigny, Henriette Valentin Lagesse. France: Nouvelles Éditions du Pacifique, 1989. 208p. map. bibliog.

Illustrated with photographs, line drawings and watercolours, this large-format book discusses the colonial and traditional architecture of Mauritius, tracing the origins of the building style back to early French settlers, and showing the development of the plantation and urban architecture of the island. Placing the architectural development of Mauritius in historical perspective, the text and many of the illustrations provide a record of the way people lived as well as an account of architectural styles no longer fashionable.

410 **Artisanat et création à l'Ile Maurice.** (Handicrafts and creativity in Mauritius.)
Jean-Claude Fleury. Paris: Fernand Nathan, 1987. 93p. maps.

A richly illustrated work which situates craft and creativity in the cultural and ethnological context of Mauritius. Crafts covered include jewellery, basket weaving, shell-painting and ship modelling.

411 **A catalogue of the objects exhibited by the colony of Mauritius at the Paris Exhibition.**
James Morris. London: W.J. Lowe, 1867. 34p.
Apart from cataloguing the exhibits, this booklet also contains a brief statistical account of the island.

412 **Maisons traditionnelles de l'Ile Maurice.** (Traditional Mauritian houses.)
Jean Louis Pagès. Rose Hill, Mauritius: Editions de l'Océan Indien, 1978. 56p.
A large-format book with accomplished drawings of the details as well as the settings and styles of Mauritius's traditional colonial architecture. It is not only handsome to look at, but is also important for its historical and descriptive background.

413 **Le Réduit.**
Louis Rivaltz Quenette. Les Pailles, Mauritius: Henri & Company, Std. Printing Establishment, 1978. 101p.
A history of Le Réduit, the Governor-General's official residence, published to coincide with the bicentenary of the rebuilidng of the 'château'. The book includes the legends that have developed about the building, and gives precise details of its construction and history, with a list of the governors and governors-general who lived there.

Regards sur la vieille cité. (Views of the old city.)
See item no. 135.

National monuments of Mauritius.
See item no. 137.

Customs, folklore and festivals

414 **Le folklore de l'Ile Maurice.** (Mauritian folklore.)
Charles Baissac. Paris: G.P. Maisonneuve & Larose, 1967. 468p.
This is a new edition of Baissac's 1888 outline of the Mauritian folklore in Creole with a French translation. Baissac's philological interests also led him to write a book about Mauritian tales (*Récits Créoles*), which was published in 1884 in Paris by H. Oudin (428p.).

415 **Pages africaines de l'Ile Maurice.** (Africa in Mauritius.)
Marcel Didier.   Rose Hill, Mauritius: Editions de l'Océan Indien,
1987. 56p.

A collection of articles tracing the African and Malagasy origins of a number of
traditional Mauritian customs such as the *sega* (the national dance). It also looks at
various children's games, forms of dress and rites which sprang from the original slave
era, with its roots in the African ancestral past.

416 **The Mauritian kaleidoscope. Languages and religions.**
Monique Dinan.   Port Louis: Best Graphics, 1986. 74p. bibliog.

This book examines languages, religions and customs against a historical background.
Analysis of the statistical information from the last four censuses (1952, 1962, 1972 and
1983) shows evolving social trends as well as the complexity of the island's social
structure.

417 **Contes de Rodrigues.** (Tales from Rodrigues.)
Jacques Edouard.   Stanley, Rose Hill, Mauritius: Editions de l'Océan
Indien, 1986. 40p.

Tales of Rodrigues told by a young Rodriguan journalist. It is written in French, with
Creole nuances. The tone is moralistic and gives an insight into that little-known island
which is part of Mauritius.

418 **The primordial link. Telegu ethnic identity in Mauritius.**
Ananda Devi Nirsimloo-Anenden.   Moka, Mauritius: Mahatma
Gandhi Institute, 1990. 182p. bibliog.

This is a treatise on Telegu ethnic identity in the island, through a study of the
community's marriage rites, kinship system and rituals, all of which make them a
distinctive group. A sociological study, it was Nirsimloo-Anenden's PhD thesis,
supervised by the School of Oriental and African Studies, University of London.

419 **Festivals of Mauritius.**
Ramesh Ramdoyal.   Rose Hill, Mauritius: Editions de l'Océan Indien,
1990. 169p.

A mixture of East and West, of Asia, Africa and Europe, of Hinduism, Christianity,
Islam and Buddhism. Mauritius is rich in its cultural diversity. The author takes us on
an exciting procession of festivals that add colour and depth to the Mauritian
experience, for all these religions and cultures live side by side and in a state of
permanent interaction. This is an introduction to a culture that succeeds in making the
reader want to know more. It is richly illustrated with colour photographs.

420 **La franc-maçonnerie à l'Ile Maurice.** (Freemasonry in Mauritius.)
Louis Rivaltz Quenette.   Port Louis: Editions La Vauverdoise, Best
Graphics Ltd., 1987. 156p. bibliog.

A study which traces back the origins of freemasonry in the island to the mid-18th
century, and describes its subsequent propagation and popularity. It considers its
philosophy, traditions and beliefs and the important personalities who practise it.

Based on original documents, the book also contributes to the history of French culture on the island in the 18th and 19th centuries.

421 **Mauritius customs and festivals.**
Harry Saminaden. Port Louis: Nalanda Press Service, 1970. 14p.
A study of Mauritian traditions and culture which emphasizes the ethnic diversity of the population.

Mauritius: stepping into the future.
See item no. 9.

L'Ile Maurice proto-historique, folklorique et légendaire. (Proto-historic, folkloric and legendary Mauritius.)
See item no. 437.

Comment vivre à L'Ile Maurice en 25 leçons. (How to live in Mauritius in 25 lessons.)
See item no. 446.

Damyanti and the treasure hunt.
See item no. 460.

More tales from Mauritius.
See item no. 462.

Music and dance

422 **Sega: the Mauritian folk dance.**
Jacques K. Lee. London: Nautilus Publishing. 1990. 105p. map.
Jacques Lee explains the origins, traditions and development of the Mauritian national music and dance form, the *sega*. There are photographs of the dance being performed and brief biographies of some of its best-known performers.

423 **Ti Frer (Little brother).**
Marcel Poinen, Jean-Clément Cangy. Mauritius: Immedia and the Centre de Documentation, de Recherches et de Formation Indienocéaniques, 1991. [n.p.].
The book is a tribute to Alphonse Ravaton, known as Ti Frer, who did much to popularise the *sega* which is the Mauritian folk-song and dance. He composed his own *segas* although he did not read music. The life-history is told in French, Creole and English.

424 **Traditional singing games of Mauritius.**
Suchita Ramdin. Moka, Mauritius: Mahatma Gandhi Institute, 1989.
60p.
One of a series of learning kits for small children on Mauritian folk culture. The book
is illustrated and accompanied by a music cassette.

Theatre

425 **Le théâtre à l'Ile Maurice: son origine et son développement.** (The
theatre in Mauritius: its origin and development.)
Antoine Chellin. Port Louis: Mauritius Printing, 1954. 109p. (Société
de l'Histoire de l'Ile Maurice, no. 5).
The theatre has always been popular in Mauritius. Antoine Chellin's historical
account, from the theatre's beginnings after the French Revolution (1789) to modern
times, fills a gap in the study of the development of art and culture in Mauritius.

Libraries and museums

426 **The Mauritius Institute Bulletin 100th anniversary 1880-1980.**
Edited by Deva Dutton Tirvengadum. *Mauritius Institute Bulletin*,
vol. 9 (Nov. 1980), Part I: Natural Sciences; Part II: National Heritage.
Under the aegis of the Mauritius Institute are included the Museum of Natural
History, the public library and the Maritime Museum of Mahébourg. Contributions to
this work are in English and French by Mauritians as well as non-Mauritians on various
aspects of the island's cultural and natural heritage. All were written in the context of
the 100th anniversary of the Institute whose mandate is 'to promote the study and
culture of the different types and aspects of art, literature, science and philosophy for
the education and entertainment of the population' ('de promouvoir l'étude et la
culture des différentes branches et aspects des arts, des sciences de la littérature et de
la philosophie, pour l'instruction et les loisirs de la population').

427 **Mauritius Institute 1880-1980.**
D.D. Tirvengadum. Port Louis: Mauritius Institute, 1980. 40p.
A brief history and account of the work of the oldest scientific and cultural institution
of Mauritius, which was created in 1880 and developed into a complex of public
libraries and museums. There is an appendix of articles published in the *Mauritius
Institute Bulletin* since 1937. There are a number of black-and-white photographs of the
buildings.

Annual report of the Archives Department.
See item no. 472.

Cuisine

428 **Cuisine simple de l'Ile Maurice.** (Simple Mauritian cookery.)
Sabita Bheekee. Quatre Bornes, Mauritius: The Author, 1984. 74p.
Mrs Bheekee provides a definitive collection of authentic Mauritian recipes, from the well-known *rougaille* to her own *poulet à la mode de 'Sab'*. A favourite recipe is *vindaye poisson*, a pickled fish dish with garlic and coarsely-ground mustard seeds. The ingredients, the amounts and their servings are indicated precisely.

429 **Genuine cuisine of Mauritius.**
G. Felix. Rose Hill, Mauritius: Editions de l'Océan Indien, 1988. 132p.
The author – a well-known Mauritian gastronome – discusses the unique cuisine of Mauritius, a blend of African, European and Asian tastes. Succulently illustrated in colour, there is a French and an English version of this book.

430 **A taste of Mauritius.**
Paul Jones, Barry Andrews. Rose Hill, Mauritius: Editions de l'Océan Indien, 1980. 180p.
A large-format, copiously illustrated book describing the diversity and richness of Mauritian cuisine. It includes many Creole, Chinese, Indian and French recipes.

431 **Exotic cuisine of Mauritius.**
Philippe Lenoir, Raymond de Ravel, translated from the French by Maryse de Broglio-Sand. Stanley, Rose Hill, Mauritius: Editions de l'Océan Indien, 1988. 299p. map.
Illustrated with colour photographs and a map of Mauritius, the main part of this book is a collection of recipes from Mauritius and some of the other Indian Ocean islands (Seychelles, Rodrigues, St. Brandon, Agaléga). Mauritian cuisine is a blend of French, Indian and Chinese cookery. An introductory section describes the ingredients and kitchen implements used in Mauritian cooking, and provides an explanation of the

local weights and measures and tropical produce available. It is followed by a brief chapter on drinking wine in the tropics.

432 Cuisinons mauricien. (Let's cook Mauritian food.)
Lalita Sookhee.   Port Louis: Proag Printing, 1989. 163p. map.

This is another book of Mauritian recipes of day-to-day dishes, made from the more readily available ingredients. There are over 300 recipes demonstrating the diversity of Mauritian cooking, a mixture of Indian, French and Chinese cuisines. The instructions are simple to follow, and there are some fish dishes worth trying. Simple illustrations accompany the descriptions.

433 Mauritian delights.
Lalita Sookhee.   Port Louis: Proag Printing, 1985. 159p. map.

Lalita Sookhee explains that Mauritian cuisine is as cosmopolitan as the people of the island, and a menu might consist of French *beignets*, English roast beef, Creole fish *rougaille* with Chinese fried rice, followed by an Indian sweet. Her collection of recipes are practical as well as colourful, and there is a guide to ingredients, spices and measures, with translations of the main Creole culinary expressions. Line drawings are included.

Literature

Fiction in French

434 Tant que soufflera le vent. (As long as the wind blows.)
Renée Asgarally. Rose Hill, Mauritius: Editions de l'Océan Indien, 1984. 209p.
The sequel to her earlier novel *Les filles de Mme. Lalljie* ('The daughters of Mrs Lalljie'), this novel is an attack on racism in Mauritius, which the author sees as an impediment to progress and freedom.

435 Brasse-au-vent. (Against the wind.)
Marcel Cabon. Rose Hill, Mauritius: Editions de l'Océan Indien, 1989. 152p.
This is an historical novel, the story of an 18th-century couple, Breton in origin, who come to Mauritius (l'Île de France) to seek their fortunes. Written with passion and style, the novel condemns the treatment given to the slaves at the time. The work is illustrated with line drawings, and is now considered a classic in Mauritian literature.

436 Namasté. (Greetings.)
Marcel Cabon. Rose Hill, Mauritius: Editions de l'Océan Indien, 1981. 96p.
A novel set in rural Mauritius, by one of the best-known Mauritian writers. The story of Ram and his family is told with sensitivity. It is a good novel for an understanding of the daily life of the Mauritian Indian immigrant. Local colour is added by the use of Creole terms.

437 **L'Ile Maurice proto-historique, folklorique et légendaire.** (Proto-historic, folkloric and legendary Mauritius.)
Malcolm de Chazal, edited by Guillemette de Spéville.   Port Louis: Mauritius Printing, 1973. 44p.

This harmonious and brilliant booklet, in French, tells of history, legends, folk-tales all mixed, the internal vision of the poet and artist, Malcolm de Chazal. The colour illustrations are a feast for the eyes.

438 **Rue La Poudrière.** (Poudrière Street.)
Ananda Devi.   Abidjan: Nouvelles Éditions Africaines, 1988. 198p.

'One city, one family, one destiny' is the theme of this novel. It is the life story of Paule in Port Louis. The emotions described are powerful and the story is told with great sensitivity. The setting is in a sleazy part of the capital.

439 **Le bal du dodo.** (The dodo ball.)
Génevière Dormann.   Paris: Editions Albin Michel, 1989. 371p.

Written by a Frenchwoman who spent some time on the island, this is a book where lightness, tenderness, irony and laughter are mixed against a background of memories, anecdotes and comments on Mauritian society.

440 **Anthologie des lettres mauriciennes.** (Anthology of Mauritian letters.)
Edited by K. Hazareesingh.   Rose Hill, Mauritius: Editions de l'Océan Indien, in collaboration with Fernand Nathan, Paris, 1978. 192p. bibliog.

A collection of selected works of Mauritian authors in English and French under the same cover. It includes biographical details of authors, as well as extracts from their works. There are poems and short stories as well as historical dissertations and essays.

441 **Anthologie poétique de Robert-Edward Hart.** (Poetic anthology of Robert-Edward Hart.)
Edited and with an introduction by K. Hazareesingh.   Moka, Mauritius: Mahatma Gandhi Institute, 1976. 128p.

The Mauritian poet Robert-Edward Hart (1891-1954) produced a number of volumes of verse, some of which were translated into English and Hindi, and acquired a number of awards for his work from the English and French governments. This volume is a selection of his poems. It is illustrated, and in French.

442 **Le naufrage du Saint Géran – Légende de Paul et Virginie.** (The wreck of St. Geran – The legend of Paul and Virginie.)
Raymond Hein.   Rose Hill, Mauritius: EOI/Fernand Nathan, 1981. 160p.

The wreck of the *St. Géran* inspired the novel of J.H. Bernardin de Saint Pierre, *Paul and Virginie* (q.v.). This book relates the circumstances leading to this disaster, and the historical details enable the reader to differentiate between legend and reality.

443 **La diligence s'éloigne à l'aube.** (The coach leaves at dawn.)
Marcelle Lagesse. Rose Hill, Mauritius: Editions de l'Océan Indien, 1985. 184p.

Lagesse is descended from a Breton family who had settled in the island in 1753. Born in 1916, she is an accomplished writer and one of the first Mauritians to produce serious novels. This tale is set in 19th-century Mauritius, when it was known as l'Isle de France.

444 **Une lanterne au mat d'Artimon.** (A lantern at the mizzenmast.)
Marcelle Lagesse. Port Louis: General Printing & Stationery, 1979. 144p.

The book tells the story of Armelle Caqueret, one of the many orphans who went to Mauritius to get married and start a new life. Mainly based on her sea voyage and first few months in the island, it is a captivating account against a background of 18th-century Mauritian society with its rules, difficulties and disillusionments. There are some beautiful, romantic illustrations done in sepia by J. Roger Merven.

445 **Le vingt Floréal au matin.** (Morning on the twentieth of November.)
Marcelle Lagesse. Cassis, Port Louis: Editions IPC, 1980. 166p.

This novel by Marcelle Lagesse is set in the Mauritius of 1799, and partly based on a true episode in history, when two French ships took refuge in the estuary of the River Noire. She relates the story of the effect this had on a family who lived in the area.

446 **Comment vivre à L'Ile Maurice en 25 leçons.** (How to live in Mauritius in 25 lessons.)
Yvan Lagesse. Route Ménagerie, Cassis, Mauritius: Editions IPC, 1980. 250p.

Amusingly illustrated with line drawings by J. Roger Merven, the author takes the reader on a highly imaginative and satirical tour of Mauritian society and culture. He gives a lot of information en route, along with various Creole interjections.

447 **Emmenez-moi à l'Île Maurice.** (Take me to Mauritius.)
Alain Le Breton. Rose Hill, Mauritius: Editions de l'Océan Indien, 1986. 208p.

The Mauritian author Alain Lebreton has written a thoughtful and elegantly-written novel which is poetic in content. It deals not only with the problems of his own country, but those of the Third World as a whole.

448 **Les noces de la vanille.** (The vanilla wedding.)
Loys Masson. Paris: Laffont, 1962. Reprinted, Rose Hill, Mauritius: Editions de l'Océan Indien, 1981. 166p.

This novel, in French, is set in the neighbouring island of La Réunion. The reprint makes available to the Mauritian public the writings of a Mauritian writer who is well-known in France. The story is evocative, and could well have happened in Mauritius.

Literature. Fiction in French

449 **Le notaire des noirs.** (The black man's notary.)
Loys Masson. Paris: Robert Laffont, 1961. Reprinted, Rose Hill,
Mauritius: Editions de l'Océan Indien, 1985. 256p.

The story of a white notary in Mauritius, descended from French settlers, who adopts a young boy called André. A novel of strong emotions, the tale describes how André comes to view his own father in a heroic light.

450 **Pigeon volé.** (The pigeon flies away.)
Berthe du Pavillon. Rose Hill, Mauritius: Editions de l'Océan Indien,
1977. 106p.

'Pigeon volé' is the name of a children's game in Mauritius – but the novel deals with adult emotions and passions. *Volé* is Creole for *s'envole* (flies away).

451 **Histoire de la littérature mauricienne de langue française.** (History of
Mauritian literature in French.)
Jean-Georges Prosper. Rose Hill, Mauritius: Editions de l'Océan
Indien, jointly with Fernand Nathan, Paris, 1978. 352p.

Of interest to the general public as well as the student of literature, this survey of the wealth of Mauritian literature in French is thoroughly researched. It traces its history back to the beginning of the 18th century, giving biographical details of poets and writers, and discusses the influence of contemporary French thinking on their work. It lists 250 authors and some 700 works.

452 **Mocélé. Anthologie de proses de Léoville L'Homme.** (An anthology of
Léoville L'Homme's prose writings.)
Vicram Ramharai. Rose Hill, Mauritius: Editions de l'Océan Indien,
1983. 90p.

A collection of stories written between 1888 and 1919 by an author who was one of the first writers to use the Creole language in his books.

453 **Pêcheurs de l'ouest.** (Fishermen of the west.)
Amode Taher. Rose Hill, Mauritius: Editions de l'Océan Indien,
1989. 138p.

A novel which deals with the tough conditions under which the fishermen of Mauritius ply their trade.

Italiques (le magazine annuel des livres). (Italics [the annual book magazine].)
See item no. 499.

Fiction in English

454 Paul and Virginie.
Jacques Henri Bernardin de St. Pierre, translated by Raymond Hein.
Rose Hill, Mauritius: EOI, 1981. 174p.

Written by Bernadin de St. Pierre, the novel depicts the tragic love story of Paul and
Virginie. It is based on true events that occurred at the time of the author's visit in
1768. See also R. Hein's *Le Naufrage du Saint Géran – Légende de Paul et Virginie*
(q.v.). A Hindi version of the well-known romance, a classic of French literature, is
also available: *Paul et Virginie (Hindi version)*, translated from the French by
B. Bissoondoyal (Rose Hill, Mauritius: Editions de l'Océan Indien, [n.d.]. 152p.).

455 The sea and man.
British Council and Club Triton. Rose Hill, Mauritius: Editions de
l'Océan Indien, 1990. 202p.

In 1987 Mauritius held an International Festival of the Sea. A short-story competition,
with the sea as the theme, was one of the events of the festival, and this book is a
collection of eleven of the stories. They show how all Mauritians are closely involved
with the sea, which inspires in them a wide range of feelings.

456 There is a tide.
Lindsey Collen. Port Louis: Ledikasyon pu Travayer, 1990. 246p.

An unusual psychological novel set in Mauritius, which includes local colour. It also
makes imaginative use of the Creole language.

457 The works of Joseph Conrad.
Joseph Conrad. London: Heinemann, 1921. 18 vols.

Twixt land and sea tales (volume 12) and *Notes on life and letters* (volume 18) include
tales on Mauritius.

458 L'île aux somnambules. (Sleepwalkers' island.)
Antelme François. Paris: Editions Acropole, 1985. 355p.

This novel describes the conflict of interest, ideologies and class in a 20th-century
fictitious island with a pluralistic society like Mauritius.

459 The return of Big Dada.
Yacoob Ghanty. Port Louis: Regent Press, 1981. 114p.

Ghanty describes his book as a socio-political novel. Set in Mauritius in 1984, it tells of
an invasion of rats led by Big Dada (Idi Amin of Uganda), and the effect of the coup
on Mauritian society.

460 Damyanti and the treasure hunt.
Hurduthlall Gungah. Rose Hill, Mauritius: Editions de l'Océan
Indien, 1986. 72p.

Two short stories in a typical Mauritian milieu, with racy dialogue, including passages
in Creole and Bhojpuri. The stories have their roots in local folklore.

119

461 **I've seen strange things: and other poems.**
Shakuntala Hawoldar.   Port Louis: The Author, 1971. 54p.

A collection of forty-four poems by the accomplished philosopher-writer who was born in India, but married a Mauritian and has spent much of her life there. The individual poems are short and have a grave, mystical beauty.

462 **More tales from Mauritius.**
Ramesh Ramdoyal.   Stanley, Rose Hill, Mauritius: Editions de l'Océan Indien, jointly with Macmillan, London, 1981. 74p.

These stories are evocative of Mauritian life, and reveal much about the people's attitudes and beliefs. See also the author's *Tales from Mauritius* (q.v.).

463 **Tales from Mauritius.**
Ramesh Ramdoyal.   Stanley, Rose Hill, Mauritius: Editions de l'Océan Indien, jointly with Macmillan, London, 1979. 80p.

All nine short stories have a Mauritian background. For a further collection, see the author's *More tales from Mauritius* (q.v.).

Fiction in Creole

464 **Vole, vole à la fête. Trois ti zozos ki ti rode vine zolis.** (Let's fly to the party. Three little birds which wanted to become beautiful.)
L'Atelier d'Art Enfantin.   Quatre Bornes, Mauritius: The Author, [n.d.]. 63p.

This collection of nineteen tales for children in a mixture of French and Creole was the result of a story competition. It brings together the best of the entries. The first tale, which gives the book its title, takes its inspiration from the place names around the island and the story is woven round it. All the stories are rich with allusions to Mauritian folklore and the natural beauties of the island, reminiscent of the tales told by the older generation to children. The book is brightly illustrated with children's drawings.

465 **Zistwar Labutik.** (The story of the shop.)
Forest Side Playgroup, Mauritius: The Federation of Pre-School Playgroups, 1986. 30p.

A simple and effectively told story for very young children written in a rhythmic way, teaching them what to expect to find in a shop and to prepare them for learning to count. The story explains that shopkeeping is work – the shop opens at seven a.m. and closes at seven p.m. – and lists the things in the shop – such as zariko ruz (red kidney beans) and bwat sardinn (tins of sardines). The shopkeepers have to get a cat to protect their shop from the mice which infest it. The book includes instructions for teachers on how to prepare their pupils for a visit to a shop.

466 **Revi Literer.** (The Literary Review.)
Edited by Richard Etienne. Grand River Northwest, Mauritius:
Sosyete Ekrivin Langaz Kreol, 1990. 24p.

An illustrated magazine of writing and poetry in the Creole language. This issue carries an interview with the Director of the Creole Institute in the Seychelles, Mme. Marie-Thérèse Choppy, about its work.

467 **La mare mo mémoire.** (From the depths of my memory.)
Ramesh Ramdoyal. Rose Hill, Mauritius: EOI, 1985. 62p.

The poet goes down memory lane in this collection of twenty poems in Creole. Enchanting, at times moving, they all have a Mauritian background with the two main themes being the abolition of slavery and immigrant Indian labour.

468 **Toufann.** (Tempest.)
Dev Virahsawmy. Rose Hill, Mauritius: Boukié Banané, 1991. 24p.

Toufann is Bhojpuri/Creole for 'tempest/storm', and this is a three-act fantasy on Shakespeare's *The Tempest*, where Prospero becomes Polonlouss, and characters like Kalibann, Aryel, Ferdjinan, Yago and Kordelia appear. Students of the Creole language would find it useful, although Sir John Gielgud would find the idiom unfamiliar.

Government Reports and Statistics

469 **Annual digest of statistics.**
Central Statistical Office, Ministry of Economic Planning and
Development. Port Louis: Government Printer, 1984–. annual.

Published annually, this report covers the important figures on the demographic,
economic and social characteristics of Mauritius – for example, population,
international travel and tourism, public health, public finance and banking, external
trade and land utilization. The 1989 digest (published June, 1990) comprised 158
pages.

470 **Government Gazette of Mauritius.**
Prime Minister's Office. Port Louis: Government Printer, 1811–.
weekly.

This contains records of all government business from the time when Mauritius became
a British colony (1810). It continues to appear regularly. In English, copies are
available at the Mauritius Archives.

471 **Indian immigration. Arrivals, births, departures and deaths from 1834
to 1st Jan 1853.**
T. Hugon. Port Louis: Immigration Department, 1853. 10p.

A comprehensive statistical compilation of Indian immigrants in the then British
colony, at a period of busy labour recruitment for the sugar plantations.

472 **Annual report of the Archives Department.**
Mauritius Archives. Port Louis: Government Printers, 1893-1922,
1949–. annual.

An account of official archival activities in Mauritius, with a supplementary
bibliography. Its bibliographical supplements dated from 1954, when Toussaint's
bibliography (q.v.) stopped, are the only consistent records of books about Mauritius
published either in Mauritius or abroad.

473   **Women in Mauritius (in figures).**
Ministry of Labour and Industrial Relations, Women's Rights and
Family Welfare.   Port Louis: The Author, 1989. 32p.

A statistical account of women's place in Mauritian society, aimed at underlining the
importance of women's contribution to economic and social development. It covers
population, birth, life expectancy, education, employment, women in politics and
social security.

474   **Report of the director of audit/for the year ended 30 June 1989.**
Port Louis: Government of Mauritius, 1990. 158p.

A comprehensive and statistical report outlining the scope of the audit and covering all
the Ministries in turn, with many tables and explanatory notes. It appears regularly at
the end of the financial year which runs from July to June.

475   **Statistique de l'Ile Maurice et ses dépendances (suivie d'une notice
historique sur cette colonie et d'un essai sur l'île de Madagascar).**
(Statistics of Mauritius and its dependencies, followed by a short history
of Mauritius and an essay on Madagascar.)
Le Baron d'Unienville.   Port Louis: *Merchants and Planters Gazette*,
(1885).

Written (in French) by the island's colonial archivist, this work, in two parts (327p.),
provides the basis for further studies on the Dutch, French and beginning of the British
periods. The first part describes in fair detail the geography, climate, soil, geology,
population, customs and economic and commercial activities. The second part relates
the history of Mauritius, together with that of Madagascar, from their origins to 1830.
Unfortunately, there is no bibliography. Only a photocopy exists in the Mauritius
Archives.

Mass Media

Newspapers

476 **Le Message.** (The Messenger.)
Ahmadiyya Muslim Association of Mauritius. Port Louis: Century Printing, 1961–. irregular.
Written for the Muslim community. In French, it is a religious as well as a cultural paper and keeps the community informed about important dates in their religious calendar.

477 **China Times (Chung Kuo Shih Pao).**
Edited by L.S. Ah Keng. Port Louis: [s.n.], 1953–. daily.
Mainly a paper for the Chinese community, written in Chinese. The Chinese are a minority in Mauritius, forming about three per cent of the close to one million population. This is one of two Chinese daily papers.

478 **Le Socialiste.** (The Socialist.)
Edited by Vedi Ballah. Port Louis: Ocean Printing, 1982–. daily.
A political paper in English and French.

479 **Week-end.**
Edited by Gerard Cateaux. Port Louis: Le Mauricien, 1966–. weekly.
A popular paper, in English and French, which carries advertisements. It also includes local and some international information.

480 **The Chinese Daily News.**
Chung Hai Fo, director.   Port Louis, 1932–. daily.
Written in Chinese, this newspaper is currently edited by Wong Yuen Moy (1991) and carries advertisements. The older of the two Chinese daily papers, it carries general news as well as items of special interest.

481 **The Sun.**
Dyanane Conhyea, director.   Port Louis: Sun Printing Ltd., 1986–. daily.
Written in English and French. A political paper, it is edited by S. Gobin.

482 **New Advance.**
Edited by James Burty David.   Port Louis: Key Publications, 1991–. weekly.
This is a new publication of comment and information, written in English and French, with politics as its key focus.

483 **La Vie Catholique.** (Catholic Life.)
Edited by Monique Dinan.   Port Louis: L'Union Catholique de l'Ile Maurice, 1930–. weekly.
A popular and respected paper, aimed mainly at the Catholic community. It is written in English and French, though French predominates. This periodical includes important dates in the religious calendar, and informs its readers about the Catholic Church's policy on serious issues such as family planning.

484 **Le Rassembleur.** (The Gatherer.)
Edited by Hervé Duval.   Swan Printing, 1986–. [Discontinued]. weekly.
A political paper, written in French. Many such papers appear at election time and then disappear. Copies are available at the City Library, Port Louis, or the Mauritius Institute.

485 **Sunday.**
Edited by Subash Gobiri.   Port Louis: Sun Printing Ltd., 1986–. weekly.
Written in English and French, this is a light-hearted Sunday newspaper. It deals mainly with local news.

486 **The Patriot.**
Edited by Teklall Gunnesh.   Les Pailles, Mauritius: Anil Kumar Proag, 1990–. weekly.
A new publication, and one of the few papers written entirely in English.

487 L'Express. (The Express.)
Edited by Yvan Martial.   Port Louis: La Sentinelle, 1963–. daily.

This is a newspaper of comment and information, written mainly in French with some articles in English. It carries advertisements and also covers births, deaths and social events. It is the only national morning paper.

488 Lumière. (The Light.)
Edited by Soon Mathuvirin.   Rose Hill, Mauritius: [s.n.], 1980–. monthly.

A cultural paper with views by the Federation of Tamil Temples. It is written in Tamil, English and French, and features the main highlights of the Tamil-speaking community.

489 The Mirror.
Edited by Ng Kee Siong.   Port Louis: Dawn Printing, 1975–. weekly.

A Sunday newspaper written in Chinese. More light-hearted in its approach than the two Chinese daily papers.

490 Le Croissant. (The Crescent.)
Edited by Bashir Ahmad Oozeer.   Port Louis: Mauritius Islamic Mission/Nimco Press, 1969–. fortnightly.

This publication is aimed at the Muslim community, and is written in English and French. It has a cultural emphasis, and is informative about Moslem rights and the Islamic world.

491 The New Nation.
Edited by Anil Ramessur.   Port Louis: Roger Valerie, 1985–. daily.

The paper's name is no indication of whether the articles would be in French or English. There are very few newspapers that are published in one language only. Known as *Nation* before it changed hands.

492 Mauritius Times.
Edited by B. Ramlallah.   Port Louis: Prakash Ramlallah Foundation, 1954–. weekly.

An independent paper of considerable repute that was first published at a time of great political activity for self-government. It is written in English and French.

493 Le Républicain. (The Republican.)
Edited by Vine Ramnauth.   Coromandel, Mauritius: Industrial Zone, 1991–. weekly.

A new paper, written in English and French. In the main, a political paper, very active at election time.

494 Challenge (Journal d'Opinion et d'Information).
Edited by N. Raya.   Beau Bassin, Mauritius: N. Raya, 1990–. weekly.

A newspaper of comment and information in English and French.

495 **Arc-en-ciel.** (The Rainbow.)
     B. Seebaluck.   Stanley, Rose Hill, Mauritius: Editions de l'Océan
     Indien, 1985–. monthly.
Written in English and French, this magazine gets its name from the diversity of races,
religions and cultures that make the Mauritian population 'a rainbow nation'.
Articles aim at nation-building, national integration and awakening of the sense of
patriotism.

496 **Le Mauricien.** (The Mauritian.)
     Edited by Sydney Selvon.   Port Louis: Le Mauricien, 1908–. daily.
An independent paper, in English and French. One of the oldest newspapers, it
appears daily in the afternoon, carrying serious items, mainly local, but with some
foreign news coverage.

497 **Swadesh.** (My country.)
     Pamplemousses, Mauritius: Proag Printing, 1986–. weekly.
The only regular newspaper written in Hindi.

Periodicals

498 **Turf Magazine.**
     Edited by Stellio Antonio, Daniel Soulange, Rashid Meerun.   Port
     Louis: Le Mauricien, 1991–. weekly.
This seasonal publication, in English and French, gives a complete guide to horse-
racing in Mauritius.

499 **Italiques (le magazine annuel des livres).** (Italics [the annual book
     magazine].)
     Edited by Issa Asgarally.   Les Pailles, Mauritius: Mauritius Stationery
     Manufacturers, 1991–. annual.
This is a serious, literary, colour magazine which deals with books and authors
worldwide. It features book reviews and articles about writers.

500 **Bar Chronicle.**
     Edited by Satyajit Boolell, Yves Hein.   Port Louis: Swan Insurance
     Co. Ltd., Anglo-Mauritius Assurance Society, 1991–. irregular.
The journal of the legal profession; in English and French. Its articles include topics
such as constitutional issues and fundamental rights.

501 **Eco – Magazine de l'Economie et des Affaires.** (Eco – Economy and Business Magazine.)
Edited by Jacques Catherine.   Port Louis, 1989–. monthly.
A business and economic magazine, in English and French.

502 **Zone Franche Magazine.** (Free Zone Magazine.)
Edited by James Clency Hurry.   Port Louis: Proag Printing, 1989–. weekly.
A magazine for the Free Zone, written in French, with only a limited circulation. Its aim is to inform workers about their rights and who to contact about grievances.

503 **Mukta.** (Liberation.)
Edited by Rajnarain Guttee.   Port Louis: Proag Printing Ltd., 1990–. monthly.
A children's Hindi magazine, promoting a sense of nationhood.

504 **Un Million de Consommateurs.** (One Million Consumers.)
Edited by Yousouf Jhugroo.   Beau Bassin, Mauritius: T-Printers, Mapbin/Chan, 1990–. monthly.
A consumers' magazine, and necessarily in French, as more people read French than English. The one million refers to the size of the island's population. This magazine deals with information about consumers' rights.

505 **Issue-based Indian Ocean Network (IBION).**
Edited by Davinder Lamba.   Port Louis: CEDREFI (Centre de Documentation, de Recherches et de Formation Indienocéaniques) & IBION Secretariat, Mazingira Institute, Nairobi, 1986–. three times per year.
This newsletter began publication in 1986, following an IBION workshop held in Mauritius the previous year and attended by delegates from ten Indian Ocean countries. The IBION newsletter appears three times a year in English and French. It can be obtained from CEDREFI, PO Box 91, Rose Hill, Mauritius.

506 **Mauritian International.**
Edited by Jacques K. Lee.   London: Nautilus Publishing, 1964–. quarterly.
Formerly *Voice of Mauritians*, this is a newspaper for Mauritians living abroad. It has news of Mauritius, and information about events of interest to Mauritians in London. It also carries advertisements, and publishes a list of books by Mauritians and others about Mauritius, that are published abroad or in Mauritius. Some of these books can be bought from *Mauritian International*, which stocks them.

507 **Indian Ocean Newsletter.**
Edited by Kenneth McPherson.   Bentley, Nedlands, Western
Australia: Western Australia Institute of Technology and the
University of Western Australia, 1979–. three times per year.
In 1979 an international conference on Indian Ocean Studies was held at Perth,
Western Australia; the *Indian Ocean Newsletter*, now published three times a year,
began publication as a result of that conference and contains a wide range of articles
about the Indian Ocean region. The newsletter can be obtained from the Director,
Centre for Indian Ocean Regional studies, Curtin University of Technology, Bentley,
6102, Western Australia.

508 **Journal of Mauritian Studies.**
Mahatma Gandhi Institute.   Moka, Mauritius: The Author, 1991–.
bi-annual.
Written mainly in English, this journal is a scholarly educational publication, reporting
on research projects such as socio-linguistic studies, Indian immigration and political
parties.

509 **Mauritius Police Magazine.**
Port Louis: Police Department, 1953–. annual.
Written in English and French, this is an in-house magazine.

510 **Racetime.**
Mauritius Turf Club.   Port Louis, 1991–. weekly during the racing
season which runs from May to November.
This is the official horse-racing programme and review magazine, in English and
French, which appears weekly in season (i.e., during the cooler 'racing' months).

511 **Al Haadi (Organe du Jamiat-Ulama de Maurice).** (The Voice of the
Jamiat-Ulama of Mauritius.)
Edited by Moufti Mohammad Raffick Meerun.   Port Louis: Best
Graphics, 1987–. monthly.
A religious magazine for the Moslem community.

512 **Le Militant Magazine.** (Militant Magazine.)
Joseph Raumiah, editor-in-chief.   Port Louis: Mouvement Militant
Mauricien, 1990–. weekly.
The official organ of the MMM (Mouvement Militant Mauricien) political party, written
in English and French.

513 **Détente.** (Leisure.)
Khalid Rawat, Diane d'Espagnac, Rémi Barrot, Cyril Espitalier-Noël,
edited by Khalid Rawal. Port Louis: Le Club Hippique de Maurice,
1990–. quarterly.
A publication of the horse-racing club of Mauritius, and therefore mainly of interest to
its adherents.

514 **La Gazette des Iles de la Mer des Indes.** (Gazette of the Indian Ocean
Islands.)
Revue d'Histoire des Îles de l'Océan Indien. Vacoas, Mauritius: The
Revue, 1986–. quarterly.
An illustrated, historical magazine, written and published in Mauritius. It is of great
interest for its varied and often scholarly content. The November 1990 (no. 58) issue
carries an edited version (by Marcelle Lagesse) of Nicolas de Céré's observations of
weather during his stay in the South of the island in 1782.

515 **Week-end Scope.**
Jacques Rivet, director. Port Louis: Le Mauricien, 1988–. weekly.
A popular magazine, with television programmes, in English and French.

516 **5-Plus – Magazine de l'Evénement et des Loisirs.** (5-Plus – The News
and Leisure Magazine.)
Finlay Salesse. Beau Bassin, Mauritius: T-Printers, 1989–. weekly.
Mainly a popular television programme and leisure magazine, written in English and
French.

517 **L'express – culture and research.**
Edited by Dev Virahsawmy. Port Louis: L'Express Newspaper, La
Sentinelle Ltée, 1991–. quarterly.
A new magazine which aims to appear quarterly. It contains articles on a variety of
subjects. Its aim is to provide a forum for the diffusion of ideas and views, contributing
to the improvement of life in Mauritius and beyond. It has a book review section, and
the March 1991 issue carried illustrations.

518 **L'Aurore.** (The Dawn.)
Edited by Paul Wu. Port Louis: Mission Catholique Chinoise de l'Ile
Maurice, 1987–. twice-monthly.
Written in English, French and Chinese, this publication is aimed at the Mauritian
Chinese community, eighty per cent of whom are Catholics.

Islander.
See item no. 373.

Education.
See item no. 406.

Government Gazette of Mauritius.
See item no. 470.

Broadcasting

519 **Broadcasting – a spectrum of change.**
Trilock Dwarka.   Port Louis: [s.n.], 1990. 57p. bibliog.
Available at the Mauritius Archives, this is a unique document analysing the problems
and prospects of television and its modern evolution in Mauritius. It also discusses the
ways in which the changes in broadcasting technology affect the developing cultural
and audio-visual patterns of the country.

Week-end Scope.
See item no. 515.

5-Plus – Magazine de l'Evénement et des Loisirs. (5-Plus-The News and
Leisure Magazine.)
See item no. 516.

Directories

520 **Africa south of the Sahara.**
London: Europa Publications, 1968–. annual.

A valuable yearly publication providing current statistical information about the countries in sub-Saharan Africa, with introductory articles on political developments and the economy. Mauritius figures as a separate entry in the country-by-country report. This is a reliable, standard and quick-reference book for an overall view. Maps and bibliographies are included in every issue.

521 **Africa who's who.**
Compiled and edited by A. Bing, Pramila Bennett (et al.). London: Africa Books, 1991. 1836p.

This book provides biographical data of some 12,000 eminent African personalities from all walks of life, arranged in alphabetical order. Mauritius is suitably represented with several entries which include politicians and businesspersons as well as academicians, senior civil servants, writers, diplomats and artists. Entries state nationality and occupation, date and place of birth, marital status and family, education, career, current occupation, publications if any, national and international honours, hobbies, special interests and current address.

522 **Makers of modern Africa.**
Edited by A. Bing, Pramila Bennett (et al.). London: Africa Books, 1991. 797p. maps.

Provides the life histories of 680 eminent Africans of the past, including some from Mauritius, who in their various ways have made their countries what they are today. National leaders such as Ramgoolam and Rozemont are among the personalities covered. Some entries are illustrated.

523 **Directory. Institutions/organisations and individuals in the Southwest Indian Ocean Islands and other French speaking countries/areas bordering the Indian Ocean.**
Documentation, Research and Training Centre of Indian Ocean Issues (CEDREFI). Rose Hill, Mauritius: CEDREFI, 1990. 261p.
This is published in French and English inside the same covers, with the financial support of the Agency for Cultural and Technical Cooperation and the Canadian High Commission. The book contains brief historical, political and economic introductions for each country, followed by a directory of institutions and individuals belonging to, or affiliated to, the organization IBION (Issue-based Indian Ocean Network). This is a document intended to introduce the members of IBION to each other; IBION also produces its own newsletter (q.v.).

524 **Encyclopédie 1988.** (1988 encyclopaedia.)
Ibrahim Dossa. Port Louis: Editions de l'Ile Maurice, 1988. 99p.
A round-up of Mauritius, the country and its people, with some social and cultural details. Human values, *savoir-vivre* and etiquette are also discussed.

525 **Who's who of Southern Africa.**
Edited by S.V. Hayes. Johannesburg: KLM Essberger, 1990/91. 679p. maps.
This is an illustrated biographical record of prominent personalities of the Southern African states, including Mauritius. The Mauritius section (p. 617-41), starts with an official guide, that is a list of ministers, top civil servants, foreign and Mauritian diplomats, and others, all stated to be from the *Government Gazette* (q.v.) of the first quarter of 1990. Then there are biographies of people covering many professions.

526 **Indian Ocean islands.**
In: *Encyclopaedia Britannica, Macropaedia.* Chicago: Encyclopaedia Britannica, 1985. p. 164-80.
An article on Mauritius covering its physical and political make-up. Maps and a bibliography are included.

527 **Directory of training resources.**
Ministry of Economic Planning and Development. Port Louis: The Ministry, 1987. 2 vols.
This is a necessary publication for manpower planning in the current context of rapid industrialization in the island. The Directory of Public Training Resources relates to the training of personnel of government and semi-governmental institutions while the other volume is a Directory of Private Training Services.

Directories

528 **Dictionnaire de biographie mauricienne/Dictionary of Mauritian biography.**
Société de l'Histoire de l'Ile Maurice.   Port Louis: The Historical Society of Mauritius, 1941–. bibliog.
Provides biographical portraits of notable Mauritians, listed alphabetically with bibliographical notes. The entries, with emphasis on leading figures before 1900 in voumes 1 to 26, may be in English or French, and are scholarly and well-researched. Further compilations are in progress.

529 **Area handbook for the Indian Ocean territories.**
Theodore L. Stoddard, William K. Carr, Daniel L. Spencer, Nancy E. Walstrom, Audrey B. Whiteley.   Washington, DC: American University, Foreign Area Studies, 1971. 132p. maps. bibliog.
Designed for use by the American military forces, this publication provides factual information about Mauritius, including sections on government, languages, education and the economy. There is a bibliography and a map of the Indian Ocean region.

Mauritius Export Directory 1989-90.
See item no. 368.

Maurice guide 1971. (Mauritius guide 1971.)
See item no. 370.

Bibliographies

530 **Mauritius bibliography.**
Compiled by Gaetan Benoit, Ronald Raimbert.   Port Louis: City
Library, City Hall, 1979.
A subject index to articles in all newspapers in Mauritius from January to June 1978.

531 **The Indian Ocean, a select bibliography of resources for study in the
National Library of Australia.**
Pauline Crawcour, Shirley Holt.   Canberra: National Library of
Australia, 1979. 172p.
A major and comprehensive bibliography compiled for the International Conference
on Indian Ocean Studies held in Perth, Western Australia in 1979. There are 6,000
entries, including several on Mauritius in the context of the Indian Ocean.

532 **Indian Ocean.**
Compiled by Julia J. Gotthold, with Donald W. Gotthold.   Oxford;
Santa Barbara, California; Denver, Colorado: Clio Press, 1988. 332p.
map. (World Bibliographical Series, vol. 85).
A wide-ranging bibliography, divided into sections such as history, ocean science,
economic resources and the Indian Ocean as a strategic military area, with an
explanatory introduction. The entries are listed in each section alphabetically by title
and of the 804 entries over a hundred either make direct reference to Mauritius or
consider the country in a regional context. There is a chronology with a general index
of authors, titles and subjects.

Bibliographies

533 International African bibliography.
David Hall. London: Mansell Publishing, 1971–. quarterly.

A quarterly list of current books, papers and articles dealing with Africa. It includes a section (since 1980) on the Indian Ocean islands, covering Mauritius as well as the other south-west Indian Ocean territories. It is compiled at the Library, School of Oriental and African Studies, London.

534 Central Western Indian Ocean bibliography.
A.J. Peters, J.F.G. Lionnet. *Atoll Research Bulletin*, no. 165 (1973). maps.

This is a special issue of the *Bulletin* which contains 322p. and 3 maps. The Mauritian islands are included in this list of some 2,000 scientific papers published between 1519 and 1971, and which deal with the former British-administered territories in the Indian Ocean. The publications are listed alphabetically, and there are indices.

535 Bibliography of Mauritius (1502-1954).
A. Toussaint, H. Adolphe. Port Louis: Mauritius Archives, 1956. 884p.

Toussaint and Adolphe were Chief Archivist and Assistant Archivist, respectively, of Mauritius. This bibliography covers printed records, manuscripts, archivalia and cartographic material. It includes sections on early imprints and private publications (1768-1954); periodicals, newspapers and serials (1773-1954); government and semi-official publications (1810-1954); publications issued abroad (1600-1954) (q.v.); manuscripts and archivalia (1598-1954); and plans, maps and charts (1502-1954). The object was 'to record as fully as possible . . . every relevant piece or set of printed, manuscript and cartographic material relative to the island of Mauritius and its dependencies from 1502 to the end of 1954'. This is indeed a thorough list.

536 Bibliography of South Asia and the strategic Indian Ocean.
Compiled by research analysts of the US Army Library. Washington, DC: Department of the US Army Library, 1973. 219p. maps.

In the main, this bibliography consists of references to research reports and articles; the emphasis is on geo-political and military strategy. There are useful sections of notes on individual territories, including Mauritius, and maps.

537 Madagascar and adjacent islands, a guide to official publications.
Julian W. Witherall. Washington, DC: Library of Congress, 1965. 49p.

This compilation includes official publications under the British administration in Mauritius up to 1965. The items are arranged by place, and there is an index.

Index

The index is a single alphabetical sequence of authors (personal and corporate), titles of publications and subjects. Index entries refer both to the main items and to other works mentioned in the notes to each item. Title entries are in italics. Numbers refer to bibliographical entries.

151

Map of Mauritius

This map shows the more important towns and other features.

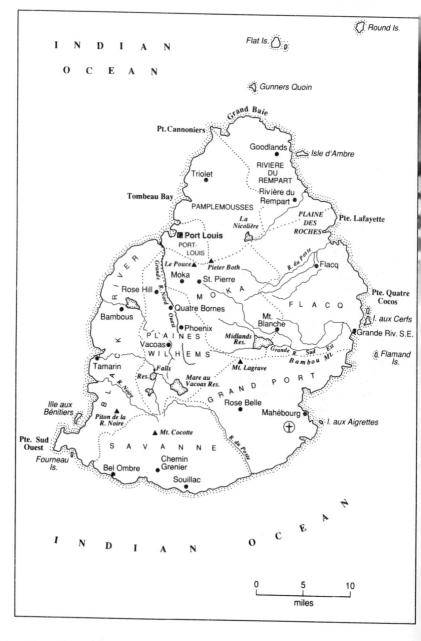

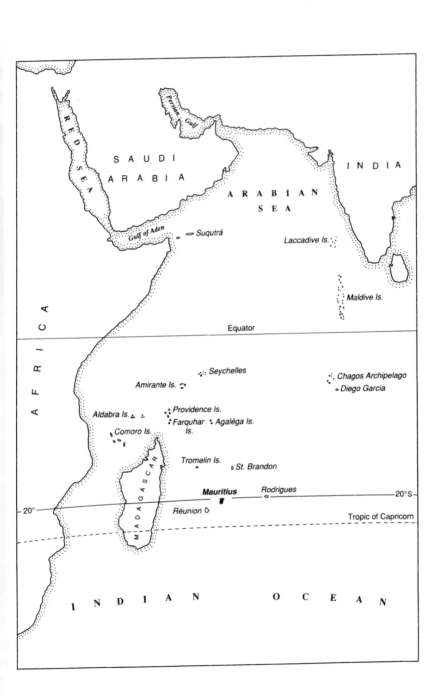